Quick Data Structures

If you want to upgrade your programming skills, the most important thing you need is a solid understanding of fundamental data structures. The proper choice of data structures distinguishes excellent programmers from merely competent ones.

As an experienced programmer, you use data structures—at least arrays—all the time. However, you may not be familiar with hash tables, trees and binary trees, priority queues, directed and undirected graphs, and other data structures at your disposal.

A good choice of data structures will simplify your job, not complicate it. Your code will be not only faster but also easier to understand and debug. There is no downside to using the right data structures for the job.

This book

- Provides an understanding of the fundamental building blocks of data structures

- Describes the construction and use of all common data structures

- Explains the simple math required for selecting efficient data structures

- Equips you with everything you need to choose data structures or devise appropriate new ones

Quick Programming Series

Most programming books are either textbooks aimed at beginners, or tomes intended to provide everything the programmer needs to know. Books in this series fulfil an important niche by offering a bridge for programmers who need a quick entry into a language, and do not need to know everything about it yet.

PUBLISHED BOOKS IN THE SERIES

Quick Data Structures

Quick Java

Quick Functional Programming

Quick JavaScript

Quick Recursion

Quick Python 3

Quick Data Structures

David Matuszek

CRC Press
Taylor & Francis Group
Boca Raton London New York

CRC Press is an imprint of the
Taylor & Francis Group, an **informa** business
A CHAPMAN & HALL BOOK

Designed cover image: 100covers.com

First edition published 2026
by CRC Press
2385 NW Executive Center Drive, Suite 320, Boca Raton FL 33431

and by CRC Press
4 Park Square, Milton Park, Abingdon, Oxon, OX14 4RN

CRC Press is an imprint of Taylor & Francis Group, LLC

© 2026 David Matuszek

For Product Safety Concerns and Information please contact our EU representative: GPSR@taylorandfrancis.com.
Taylor & Francis Verlag GmbH, Kaufingerstraße 24, 80331 München, Germany.

ISBN: 978-1-041-03813-9 (hbk)
ISBN: 978-1-041-03810-8 (pbk)
ISBN: 978-1-003-62550-6 (ebk)

DOI: 10.1201/9781003625506

Typeset in Minion
by codeMantra

*To all my students
past, present, and future*

Contents

Preface

M ANY YEARS AGO, A friend came to me with a problem.

Back then, you typed your program on punched cards and put them in a tray along with other programs to be run. Some hours later, you would get the printed results.

My friend's problem was that his program was taking more than 20 minutes to run on the Control Data 6600, which (in those days) was the world's fastest computer. According to the Computation Center rules, any program that took more than 20 minutes would be stopped and not run again until the weekend when the computer was less busy. My friend asked me if I could speed up his program.

The program was doing a lot of table look-ups, using an ordinary array. I replaced the array with a hash table–a change which reduced the running time to under 20 seconds. My friend didn't fully trust my work because, as he later told me, he spent the entire weekend hand-checking the results.

Times have changed, and today's computers are orders of magnitude faster than the "supercomputers" of yesteryear. That same program would, today, run in a few milliseconds.

Today's computers are so fast and have so much memory that, for most programs, it doesn't make sense to worry about efficiency. However, there are important exceptions: video games, popular websites, deep learning, weather modeling, and more. Besides, why struggle with a poor choice of data structures when there might be one perfectly suited to your needs?

Author

I'M DAVID MATUSZEK, KNOWN to most of my students as "Dr. Dave."

I wrote my first program on punched cards in 1963 and immediately got hooked.

I taught my first computer classes in 1970 as a graduate student in computer science at the University of Texas in Austin. I eventually earned a PhD there, and I've been teaching ever since. Admittedly, I spent over a dozen years in industry, but even then I taught as an adjunct for Villanova University.

I finally left the industry and joined the Villanova faculty full time for a few years before moving to the University of Pennsylvania, where I directed a master's program (MCIT, Master's in Computer and Information Technology) for students transitioning into computer science from other disciplines.

Throughout my career, my main interests have been in artificial intelligence (AI) and programming languages. I've used a *lot* of programming languages.

I retired in 2017, but I can't stop teaching, so I'm writing a series of "quick start" books on programming and programming languages. I've also written three science fiction novels—*Ice Jockey*,

All True Value, and *A Prophet in Paradise*—and I expect to write more. Check them out!

And, hey, if you're a former student, drop me a note. I'd love to hear from you!

david.matuszek@gmail.com

Where's the Code?

THIS ISN'T A RECIPE book. If you want the code for, say, a merge sort, you can do a web search and find code for a merge sort in any of the couple dozen most common languages. Instead, the goal of this book is to explain (for example) *how* a merge sort works, and *when* and *why* you might want to use one. Once you understand that, you can write your own or grab one of the many published versions.

Code isn't always the best way to explain an algorithm or data structure—but sometimes it is. In such cases, the code should be as readable as possible.

It's generally agreed that Python is the most readable language, but every language has glitches. Python's for loop is

```
for i in range(0, n):
 # do something
```

and it isn't necessarily obvious to a non-Python programmer that this means:

```
for i from 0 up to but not including n {
 # do something
}
```

Similarly, Python has dictionaries, "lists," and sets, which we will try to avoid. Consequently, the code in this book is "Python-like" but, in the interest of making code as readable as possible for everyone, not necessarily "real" Python.

There is one feature we retain from Python. Good programming style demands that code be indented properly, and in Python, this is a *requirement*, not just a style rule. In this book, indentation is used to indicate code controlled by an if or while statement, making braces unnecessary.

CHAPTER 1

Building Blocks

A DATA STRUCTURE IS A way of organizing information so that it can be retrieved and updated quickly and easily.

Any data structure can be created from just three basic components: arrays, nodes, and pointers.

A *node* is a (generally small) collection of named *fields* that hold data values. Nodes may be of varied types and sizes, may be arbitrarily complex, and often contain links to other nodes. For example, a node used to represent a customer may have a field named customerId to hold a unique integer, a field named email to hold a link to an email address represented as a string, and a field named orderHistory that holds a link to another node type whose values represent an order history.

In object-oriented languages, a node is almost always represented by an object, but any method of associating the various pieces of information can be made to work.

A *pointer* (also called a *reference* or a *link*) provides access to a data value that is located elsewhere in memory. Originally, a pointer was an address in physical memory, and it can still be thought of that way.

An *array* is a linear sequence of values, all of the same type and size. Because all the values are the same size, the array can be efficiently *indexed*—the location in memory of the n-th element is simply the starting location of the array plus n times the element size.

> **Note:** When an array *appears* to have elements of varying sizes (e.g., an array of strings), each value in the array is actually a link to the actual data (a string). This link is exposed to the programmer in some languages, while other languages limit access to it.

These three elements can be combined into an uncountable number of data structures. For the student, this means that there are a great many common data structures to be studied; however, the underlying concepts are simple, and new data structures can easily be invented as needed.

1.1 POINTERS AND REFERENCES

A *link* is almost always implemented as an address of some location in memory. This could be an *absolute address*, based on the physical memory of the computer, or (much more likely) it could be a *relative address*, based on the location in memory occupied by the program. Either way, an address is implemented as an integer value.

The difference between a pointer and a reference is that a *pointer* exposes its integer value to the programmer, who can then perform arithmetic on it, resulting in a pointer to a new location in memory. Pointers are common in the C family of languages.

Pointers raise security concerns. Unless handled with extreme care, they can allow malicious code to be loaded as data and then executed.

A *reference* can be stored and duplicated like any other data value, it can be *dereferenced* to get the item it points at, and two references can be compared for equality. No other operations are provided. Because the integer implementation is hidden, references are inherently more secure than pointers and require less syntax. This is how links are handled in Java, Python, and most other modern languages.

1.2 ARRAYS

An *array* is a deceptively simple data structure. It's just a linear sequence of values, generally all of the same type. To *index* into it, the language simply adds the index value times the element size to the starting location, giving the desired memory location. Indexing is a very fast operation.

There are minor variations. Depending on the language, the first location might have an index of 0, an index of 1, or some integer chosen by the programmer. Some languages allow discrete data types, such as characters, to be used as indices.

Usually, the size of the array is defined when it is created and cannot later be changed. Again, this is language-dependent.

Some languages (Fortran, for example) allow arrays to have two or more dimensions. It may be important to know the order in which values are stored (rows first or columns first), because some operations will depend on this ordering.

In any language based on C, all arrays are one-dimensional, but the values in the array may themselves be arrays. In these languages, the size of an array is not a part of its type, so arrays within an array are not all required to be the same size; if they are of differing sizes, the result is called a *ragged array*.

Finally, an array is usually implemented as more than just a sequence of values. Java, for instance, stores the array length and the element type along with the array values.

1.3 STRING ARRAYS

A *string* is a sequence of characters. Strings are almost always implemented as arrays, with one character per array location. Some languages expose the implementation, allowing a string to be accessed like any other array, while other languages hide the implementation but provide a host of functions for working with them.

To index efficiently into an array, all the values in the array must be the same size. Since strings may be of different sizes, there is really no such thing as an "array of strings." Such an array actually contains *pointers* to strings; the strings themselves are stored elsewhere. See Figure 1.1.

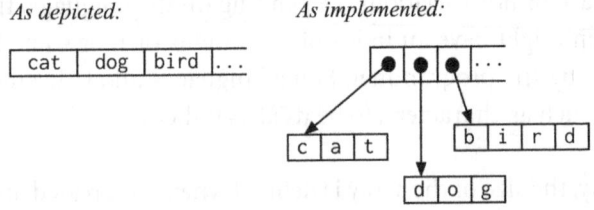

FIGURE 1.1   String array implementation.

The same is true when a node is depicted as containing a string: The node actually contains a pointer to the string.

Strings are almost always stored in a data structure called a *heap* (see Chapter 9). Heaps have the ability to hold data of varying sizes.

CHAPTER 2

Essential Math

YOU CANNOT IGNORE MATH when studying data structures. It doesn't require much math, and you don't need to solve complex equations. There are only two things required of you:

- First, you need to understand that some growth rates are better or worse than others (e.g., exponential growth is much worse than linear growth).

- Second, you need to be able to *analyze* a program to determine which kind of growth occurs as the amount of data increases. This is (usually) much simpler than it sounds.

In general, we would like to know

- How much memory is required by the program?

- How long will the program take to run?

This chapter covers all the mathematics necessary for a basic understanding of how to determine these factors. Along the way, several popular sorting algorithms are described.

DOI: 10.1201/9781003625506-2

It is very unusual for algorithms to require explosive amounts of memory, but quite common for them to demand excessive amounts of time. For this reason, our analyses are primarily about running time.

After reading this chapter, you will understand what "Big-O" notation is all about.

2.1 THE IMPORTANCE OF EFFICIENCY

There are two contradictory views that can be taken on the matter of efficiency. Although contradictory, each is correct—in the proper context.

On the one hand, computers are literally millions of times faster than they were a few decades ago. Back then, computers were expensive, while human labor was (relatively) cheap. It was important to get value out of every machine cycle. Today, however, the economics are completely reversed, and it is—to put it gently—unwise to spend an hour of a programmer's time to save a millisecond of computer time. For a large majority of programs, efficiency simply *is not and should not be* a concern.

On the other hand, there are situations in which efficiency is essential. Some examples are video games, large simulations of complex systems such as weather patterns, artificial intelligence, and very heavily used websites. Using the proper data structure can often make a program hundreds of times faster, usually with little or no additional programming effort.

The bottom line is: The effective programmer knows when to spend effort on making a program more efficient and when not to. Knowledge of data structures is the key to doing this.

2.2 ANALYSIS OF ALGORITHMS

An **algorithm** is a well-defined, step-by-step procedure that is guaranteed to terminate. There are literally thousands of published algorithms.

To **analyze** an algorithm means:

- developing a formula for predicting how fast an algorithm is, based on the size of the input (**time complexity**) and/or

- developing a formula for predicting how much memory an algorithm requires, based on the size of the input (**space complexity**).

Usually, time is our biggest concern because many algorithms require a fixed amount of space.

Since the formula depends on the "size" of the input, we need some measure of the size, and that depends on the nature of the problem.

- When searching an array, the "size" of the input could be the size of the array.

- When merging two arrays, the "size" could be the sum of the two array sizes.

- When computing the nth Fibonacci number or the nth factorial, the "size" is n.

The "size" should be a parameter that can be used to calculate the actual time (or space) required. It is frequently obvious what this parameter is, but sometimes some experimentation may be required. Sometimes we need two or more parameters—for instance, if we are dealing with a two-dimensional array where the rows and columns are treated very differently.

Of course, a program doesn't usually do just one thing. Maybe it sorts an array as just one part of a complicated series of operations. Some of those operations may take far more time (or far less time) than sorting the array. How do we put all this together to compute a "total" running time?

The short answer is, we simplify. We simplify *a lot*.

If one part of the program takes linear time and another part takes quadratic time, we completely ignore the linear part and say the program takes quadratic time. For small problems, the linear part might take longer than the quadratic part, but small problems don't take very long anyway. For large problems that require large amounts of time, the quadratic part will completely overshadow the linear part.

We might like to find the *average* time to perform an algorithm.

Unfortunately, that usually isn't well-defined. We will consider several sorting algorithms, and for most of them, the actual time they take is determined by how out of order the array is. But—how out of order is the "average" array? The question is essentially unanswerable.

We usually have to be satisfied with finding the *worst* (longest) time required, and sometimes this is even what we want (e.g., for time-critical operations). Big-O notation is all about how to simplify the estimated worst-case time (or space) requirements.

2.3 CONSTANT TIME

An operation takes **constant time** if there is some constant k such that this operation never takes more than k nanoseconds (or seconds, or whatever measure you wish to use). That is, there is a strict limit on how long the operation can take.

Here are some things that take constant time:

- Any standard arithmetic or Boolean operation.

- A call to a method that takes constant time.

- An if statement, where the test takes constant time and each branch (true or false) takes constant time.

- A switch statement, where each case takes constant time.

Notice that for an if or switch statement, the possible branches don't have to take the *same* amount of time, just that each takes no more than k time, for some constant k.

Here are some things that *probably* take more than constant time:

- A loop.

- A call to a complex or recursive method.

An operation that takes constant time k is said to be O(1), that is, "Big-O of one." Notice that we don't care how big the constant k is.

2.4 LINEAR TIME

An operation takes **linear time** if doubling the amount of data doubles the running time. Or, if tripling the amount of data triples the running time. In general, multiplying the size of the data set by n multiplies the running time by n.

Summing up the elements of an array of size n is a linear operation. Searching an array to find the largest or the smallest element is a linear operation. Counting up to n and doing something that takes constant time for each number is also linear time.

You might notice that some operations, such as adding up all the numbers in an array, are not *exactly* doubled if you double the size of the array. That's true; it takes some small amount of time to set up the loop. So the actual time required to sum up an array of n numbers is c+kn, where c is the (constant) amount of time required to set up the loop and k is the (constant) amount of time required to add each element. This expression is *linear* in n. The Big-O notation for an expression linear in n is O(n). Notice that we don't care about the size of c or k; they are just constants, so we ignore them.

2.5 QUADRATIC TIME

Many array sorting methods require **quadratic time**; that is, if the array size is increased by a factor of n, then the time required to sort that array goes up by a factor of n^2. An array ten times larger takes a hundred times longer to sort.

Here we will briefly consider three such sorting algorithms. They are of interest because they are easy to implement, because they illustrate how to informally determine the Big-O running time of an algorithm, and because they can be used to describe the important concept of a *loop invariant*.

> **Note:** We refer to the "first" and "last" indices in the array because many programming languages use zero as the smallest index, several languages use one, and some languages allow an arbitrary starting index.

2.6 BUBBLE SORT

A *bubble sort* proceeds as follows:

- Set some variable limit to the index of the last element in the array and set a flag variable swapped to true.

- While limit is greater than the first index and swapped is true:

  - Set swapped to false.

- For index i ranging from the first index in the array up to and including limit-1:
  - If array[i] > array[i+1], swap the two values and set swapped to true.
- Subtract 1 from limit.

While we generally think of using loops to *change* things (e.g., sorting an array), an equally valid view is that loops keep some condition **invariant**. An invariant is some condition that remains true even when the variables in the condition change their values.

For a bubble sort, the loop invariant is: *All array locations greater than* limit *are correctly sorted and in their final location.* This is true initially because there *are* no locations greater than limit. After one pass through the while loop, limit is reduced by one, and the value in the last array location is the largest value. After the second pass, limit has been reduced again, and the last two array elements are correctly placed. And so on. At the end, all elements are sorted.

In bubble sort, the while loop is executed up to n times, where n is the size of the array. (It could be fewer if no swaps occur, but as usual, we're interested in the worst case.) The inner for loop is initially executed n-1 times, but each time the number of executions is reduced, so on average it is executed about n/2 times. Dropping the constants, the outer loop is executed n times, and for each of those times, the inner loop is executed n times, so the overall running time is n times n, or $O(n^2)$.

The actual running time of bubble sort depends on the initial state of the array. For a random array, the expected running time is quadratic, but bubble sorting an array that is already in sorted order takes only $O(n)$ time.

Although bubble sort has the same Big-O running time as insertion sort and selection sort, it is generally the slowest of the three. There is another reason to avoid it: Bubble sort is the sorting technique most often invented by beginners, so it has a bad reputation as amateurish.

2.7 CHARACTERISTIC OPERATIONS

In computing time complexity, one good approach is to count **characteristic operations**. A characteristic operation is an operation that occurs at least as often during the execution of an algorithm as any other operation, so the number of times this operation occurs determines the Big-O running time of the algorithm.

Sorting algorithms essentially do two things: compare two values and swap two values. At each step, swaps may or may not occur, but comparisons will always occur. Therefore, comparisons make a good characteristic operation; swaps do not.

Bubble sort proceeds in a series of n passes, where n is the size of the array. The average length of each pass, L, is $n/2$. During each of those passes, L **comparisons** are made. Therefore, n passes times $n/2$ comparisons equals $n^2/4$, or $O(n^2)$.

> **Note:** The careful reader will notice that all the values mentioned in the previous paragraph are approximate. For example, the number of passes made during a bubble sort is $n-1$, not n. The important point is that these simplifications do not affect the conclusion that the running time is $O(n^2)$.

For most sorting algorithms, the number of comparisons made is a suitable choice for the characteristic operation because it controls all the other actions. Other types of algorithms require a different choice of characteristic operation.

If the algorithm has an innermost loop, we might just look at how many times that loop is executed. If a single pass through that loop takes constant time, the loop itself can be considered a characteristic operation.

2.8 INSERTION SORT

For *insertion sort*, we'll approach things a bit differently by starting with the loop invariant and using it to develop the algorithm. Here it is: *The first n elements of the array are in sorted order.*

The invariant for insertion sort differs from that of bubble sort in two respects. First, we're moving elements to the beginning of the array, rather than to the end. This is minor, and either algorithm could be adjusted to work from the other end. The second difference is important: The elements are sorted *with respect to one another* but can still be moved about; they may not be in their final positions.

To begin, notice that when we consider only the first value, it is trivially true that it is in sorted order.

Now suppose that the first k values are in sorted order. What about the next value, at location k+1? If it is at least as large as the immediately preceding value, it can remain where it is. Otherwise, we can take that value out of location k+1 and insert it somewhere earlier. We can use a binary search (see Section 2.11) to find where among the first k values it should be inserted, and we can move all the values between that location and location k up one space. Conveniently, the value that was in location k can be moved to location k+1, which has just been vacated.

Analysis: We run once through the outer loop, giving a factor of n. Each time, we perform a binary search (which takes $log(n)$ time) and then move, on average, $n/4$ elements, so that each time through the outer loop the work required is $log(n)+n$. (It's $n/4$

because we move, on average, half of the already sorted values, which is, on average, half of the total values.) We ignore constants, so the result is $n\times(log(n)+n)$, or $n\times log(n)+n^2$. Finally, $n\times log(n)$ grows more slowly than n^2, so our final result is $O(n^2)$.

Often, we are sorting not just numbers but objects according to some *key* value. A *stable sort* is one that does not change the order of objects with equal keys. For example, if we are sorting customers by name and "John Smith" from New York comes before "John Smith" from Boston, those objects should remain in the same order after sorting.

Insertion sort is a stable sort.

2.9 SELECTION SORT

Selection sort is probably the easiest to describe. Here's how it works:

Search the entire array to find the smallest value. Swap it with the value in the first location. Search the array starting from the second location to find the smallest remaining value and swap it with the value in the second location. Search the array starting from the third location to find the smallest remaining value and swap it with the value in the third location. And so on.

At each step, we search the unsorted part of the array for the smallest value and swap it with the value just past the sorted part, so the sorted part gets larger by one value.

Ignoring constants, we perform n searches, and each search examines n elements, so the running time is $O(n^2)$.

The loop invariant is that the first k elements are sorted and in their final position, as k varies from 1 to the size of the array.

2.10 EXPONENTS AND LOGARITHMS

If you are familiar with logarithms, you can skip this section.

Exponentiation, or ***raising a number to a power***, is the process of multiplying several copies of that number together. For example, 10^3, or "ten raised to the power of 3," means three tens multiplied together: $10 \times 10 \times 10 = 1000$. The number that is multiplied by itself (in this example, 10) is called the ***base***.

Taking the logarithm of a number is the inverse process: Given a number and a base, how many copies of the base must be multiplied together to get the number? In our example, three tens must be multiplied together to get 1000, so the logarithm of 1000 (base 10) is 3. We write this as $\log_{10} 1000 = 3$.

A shorthand phrase for remembering this is: "Logarithms are exponents." That is, if $x = b^n$, then $\log_b x = n$.

Logarithms are not necessarily whole numbers. The logarithm (base 10) of 1001 is slightly more than 3 (in fact, it's about 3.000434), while the logarithm (base 10) of 999 is slightly less than 3 (about 2.99957).

Any positive number may be used as the base. Here are the three most commonly used kinds of logarithms:

- ***Common logarithms*** are those that use 10 as a base; these are often encountered in engineering.

- ***Natural logarithms*** use the number *e* (approximately 2.718281828459045) and are favored by mathematicians.

- ***Binary logarithms*** use 2 as a base and are favored by computer scientists.

The various logarithms differ only by a constant factor. In particular, the binary logarithm of a number is approximately 3.322 times the common logarithm of that number. Since the common logarithm of 1000 is 3, the binary logarithm of 1000 is approximately 3.322 × 3, or 9.966.

Here's a convenient way to think about binary logarithms: *Given a number, how many times do you have to cut it in half to get to 1?*

Starting with the number 64, repeated halving gives 32, 16, 8, 4, 2, and 1. That's six halvings to get to exactly 1, so $\log_2 64$ is 6.

Things won't usually work out this exactly. Starting with 60 instead of 64, we get the sequence 30, 15, 7.5, 3.75, 1.875, and 0.9375. This tells us that five halvings (1.875) isn't enough, but six halvings (0.9375) is slightly less than 1, so the binary logarithm must be between 5 and 6, and closer to 6. (The true value is about 5.907.)

This idea of "cutting in half" will occur quite often in our discussion of algorithm timing.

2.11 BINARY SEARCH

Binary search is an algorithm for searching a sorted array for a particular value.

In a binary search, you only search the array between two indices—we'll call them left and right. These indices are initially the lowest and highest possible indices, and they will gradually move toward each other. If the item is not in the array, the indices will cross, and left will become greater than right.

Assuming the array is sorted in increasing order, the algorithm is as follows:

- If left is greater than right, return failure; the item is not in the array.

- Compute mid as the (integer) average of left and right.

- If array[mid] is the sought-after item, return mid.

- If array[mid] is too large, recursively search between left and mid-1;

- Otherwise, array[mid] is too small, so recursively search between mid+1 and right.

At each point we either find the item and return, or we recursively search half the remaining elements. Since we are eliminating half the remaining elements each time, the required time is actually *binary* logarithmic time (logarithms to the base 2), which we *could* write as $O(\log_2 n)$. Recall, however, that it doesn't matter which base we use, as the results only differ by a constant. Since we ignore constants, we write logarithmic time simply as $O(\log n)$.

The recursive binary search requires *four* parameters—the item to be sought, the array, and the additional parameters left and right. It would be nice not to have to explain those additional parameters to the user. We can avoid this with the use of a façade function:

> **Terminology:** A *façade* function is a function whose only job is to provide a nicer interface to the function that does the actual work.

In this example, the façade function will take only two parameters: the item sought and the array. It will then determine the appropriate initial values for left and right and make a single call to the recursive function.

In some languages, the façade function and the recursive function can have the same name. In other languages, different names are required, and the façade function should have the more user-friendly name. If the programming language allows functions to be nested, the recursive version can be "hidden" inside the façade function.

2.12 QUICKSORT

The *quicksort* algorithm is one of the fastest sorting algorithms known. It is a *recursive algorithm*—that is, the quicksort method calls itself.

Here's the basic idea:

- Some number from the array is chosen as a *pivot*.

- The array is *partitioned* into two parts. The numbers less than the pivot are moved to the left side of the array, while the numbers greater than or equal to the pivot are moved to the right side of the array.

- The smaller numbers in the left partition are quicksorted, and independently, the larger numbers in the right partition are quicksorted.

  - If the size of the partition (the right index minus the left index) is zero or one, the recursion "bottoms out," and that partition is fully sorted.

The top-level quicksort method itself is practically self-explanatory. Here is the complete method (in Python):

```
function quicksort(array, left, right):
    if left < right:
        p = partition(array, left, right)
        quicksort(array, left, p)
        quicksort(array, p + 1, right)
```

The initial test (left < right) checks whether anything more needs to be done. The initial call will be with the entire array, so left will be zero (in most languages), and right will be the size of the array minus one. If quicksort is called with left greater than or equal to right, the partition size is zero or one, and this branch of the recursion is finished.

The partition method moves smaller numbers to the left, larger numbers to the right, and returns the index p of the rightmost small number. How this is done will be explained after the following example.

- Start with the array [68, 81, 20, 50, 60, 78, 47, 90].

- If we take 68 as the pivot, we can partition the array into two parts: [47, 60, 20, 50 | 81, 78, 68, 90]. The first part contains the numbers less than 68, while the second part contains the numbers greater than or equal to 68. Neither part is sorted.

- Quicksort the left part, [47, 60, 20, 50].

    - Taking 47 as the pivot, we partition this into the two parts [20 | 60, 47, 50].

    - The [20] part consists of a single number, so no further sorting is necessary.

    - [60, 47, 50] can be partitioned into [50, 47 | 60], using 60 as the pivot.

    - The [50, 47] part requires another quicksort step, but the [60] part does not.

    - The initial left partition is now completely sorted.

- Quicksort the right part, [81, 78, 68, 90].

    - Taking 81 as the pivot, this can be partitioned into [68, 78 | 81, 90].

- The two parts of [68, 78 | 81, 90] can each be quick-sorted (to no effect, since they are already in the correct order).

- The initial right partition is now completely sorted.

The partition method works as follows. Given an array segment to be partitioned, choose some value in the array segment to serve as a pivot. In the above example, we always chose the leftmost value in the array. Then search from the left end for a value greater than or equal to the pivot, and search from the right for a value less than the pivot. If the left index is still less than the right index, swap the two values.

With this array segment, using 68 as the pivot, the search from the left finds 68, while the search from the right finds 50.

```
[68, 81, 20, 47, 60, 78, 50, 90]
 →                        ←
```

Swapping these two values, we get

```
[50, 81, 20, 47, 60, 78, 68, 90]
```

Continuing the searches from where we left off (just to the right of the 50 and just to the left of the 68), we find 81 as greater than 68, and 60 as less than 68.

```
[50, 81, 20, 47, 60, 78, 68, 90]
     →            ←
```

Swapping these two values gives us

```
[50, 60, 20, 47, 81, 78, 68, 90]
```

Continuing the searches from where we left off (just to the right of the 60 and just to the left of the 81), we find 81 as the first number greater than 68, and 47 as the first number less than 68.

```
[50, 60, 20, 47, 81, 78, 68, 90]
          ←  →
```

At this point, the left index has become greater than (or equal to) the right index, so the partition operation is finished; the numbers 50 to 47 are all less than 68, and the numbers 81 to 90 are all greater than or equal to 68. The index of 47 (the rightmost number in the left partition) is returned as p, the value of the partition method.

That's the complete algorithm.

In the above example, we took the first value in each array segment as the pivot. Other options include picking the value in the center of the array segment and picking a random value in the array segment. Each approach may have some minor advantages.

Quicksort is faster than insertion sort for large arrays, but for small arrays (up to 10 or 12 elements), insertion sort is faster. For this reason, a hybrid sort is sometimes implemented, where small partitions are sorted using insertion sort. This additional effort is probably worthwhile for a library routine to be used by the general public.

2.13 ANALYZING QUICKSORT

Quicksort is a recursive algorithm. To analyze it—that is, to determine its running time—we need to know two things: the running time of the partition method, and the depth of the recursion. Multiplying these two numbers together will give us the result.

To partition the entire array, we find a large number from the left end, a small number from the right end, and swap them. Every element of the array is compared to the pivot once and possibly swapped with another element. The comparison and the possible swap each take constant time, and there are n elements in the array, so to partition the entire array takes $O(n)$ time.

But that's just for the first level of partitioning. What about the second level? In our example, the array was split in half, but each partition operation had half as much to do, so $\frac{1}{2}O(n) + \frac{1}{2}O(n) = O(n)$. If the array were split differently, it would still work out: $\frac{1}{3}O(n) + \frac{2}{3}O(n) = O(n)$. We can conclude that $O(n)$ work is done at each depth of the recursion.

The depth of the recursion in this example is 3. We started with an array of size 8, cut it into two pieces each of size 4, cut those into pieces of size 2, and cut those into pieces of size 1. Thus, we cut the array in half three times to get to a size of 1. In terms of logarithms, $\log_2(8) = 3$. More generally, we can expect quicksort to have a recursive depth of $\log_2(n)$ for an array of size n.

Initial conclusion: Quicksort has a running time of $O(n \times \log(n))$, usually written as just $O(n \log n)$, where n is the size of the array.

While our initial conclusion is basically correct, there are caveats. Our example was chosen so that each partition operation split the part being sorted into equal halves; this is the best case. For a random array, the expected size of the division is roughly $\frac{1}{3}$ and $\frac{2}{3}$. This isn't as neat, but a careful analysis still results in an expected running time of $O(n \log n)$.

The worst case occurs when every partition operation splits an array segment of size n into a segment of size 1 and a segment of size n-1. The depth of the recursion is then $O(n)$ instead of $O(\log n)$, and $O(n)$ times $O(n)$ gives quicksort a running time of $O(n^2)$.

Unfortunately, the worst case will occur when the pivot is chosen to be the first element (or the last element) in the array segment, and the array is already sorted. The amount of work done at each level of the recursion is still $O(n)$, but the maximum depth of the recursion, instead of being $\log(n)$, is now n. In this case, quicksort takes $O(n^2)$ time.

There are a couple of ways to avoid this. You can do a pre-check to make sure the array isn't already sorted; or you can choose the middle element rather than the end element of the array segment; or you can choose a random element in the array segment. Other approaches are possible and almost always work, but there is no way to absolutely guarantee that quicksort won't take $O(n^2)$ time.

Final conclusion: Quicksort *almost always* has a running time of $O(n \log n)$, where n is the size of the array, but there is no guarantee that it won't take $O(n^2)$ time. Therefore, quicksort should not be used in critical applications where an $O(n \log n)$ running time is an absolute requirement.

When $O(n \log n)$ running time *is* a requirement, **merge sort** is a good alternative.

2.14 MERGE SORT

Merge sort, like quicksort, is a recursive algorithm. Like quicksort, at each level of the recursion, it divides the array into two parts. Unlike quicksort, however, the two parts are always of approximately equal size, thus guaranteeing $O(n \log n)$ running time. Here's how it works:

- Copy half the numbers into a new array, and the remaining numbers into a second new array. (If the array size is odd, one array will be slightly larger than the other.)

- Independently merge sort the two smaller arrays. If an array size is 0 or 1, it is already sorted.

- *Merge* the two arrays by repeatedly comparing the smallest numbers in each and copying the smaller back into the original array. When all numbers in either array have been copied, copy any remaining numbers in the other array.

For example, we will start with the array A = [56, 1, 44, 17, 24, 60, 71, 51]. Copy the two halves of this array into new arrays B and C, so B = [56, 1, 44, 17] and C = [24, 60, 71, 51].

Merge sort B to get [1, 17, 44, 56].

Merge sort C to get [24, 51, 60, 71].

Finally, merge B and C back into array A. See Figure 2.1.

```
B: [ 1, 17,     44, 56]
     ↓  ↓       ↓   ↓
C: [ ↓  ↓  24,  ↓   ↓   51, 60, 71]
     ↓  ↓  ↓    ↓   ↓   ↓   ↓   ↓
A: [ 1, 17, 24, 44, 56, 51, 60, 71]
```

FIGURE 2.1   Merging two arrays.

Merge sort is much slower than quicksort on average but has a guaranteed running time of O(n log n). Like quicksort, it can be sped up by switching to an insertion sort for smaller arrays.

Merge sort is not an in-place sort, so it requires additional storage. Since each recursion cuts the size of the array in half, recursions will proceed to a depth of O(log n). Memory requirements would therefore seem to be O(n log n), but this is incorrect.

As long as the code is executed sequentially (not in parallel), the extra space is ½n for the first level of recursion, then ½(½n) = ¼n for the second level, then ½(¼n) = ⅛n, and so on; the sum of these is O(n).

So while O(n log n) space may be required in total, only O(n) space is required at any one time.

2.15 EVEN FASTER SORTS

The best sorts we have seen so far have running times of O(n log n). Is it possible to do better?

You will often see that the answer is "no." The proof is based on the fact that an array of *n* values can be arranged in *n!* ways, and to sort these out requires *n×log(n)* decisions.

But that proof assumes that all values may be distinct. In this section, we will discuss two sorting algorithms, each of which requires only O(n) time.

Algorithm 1

Suppose you have an array of a thousand scores, where each score is in the range 0 to 25. All you need to do is set up an array of 26 locations (0 to 25), zero out the array, and for each score, add 1 to the corresponding location of your array of counts. After all scores have been tallied, you can put these scores back into the original array.

Of course, each score probably has associated information, such as who made that score. That complicates the bookkeeping but doesn't affect the running time, which is O(n).

This is a special case because there are only a small, finite number of scores.

Algorithm 2

Back when programs were typed onto punched cards, one line of text per card, the last 8 columns of each card were reserved for a *card number*. The idea was that if your cards were numbered, and you dropped the deck, they could be put in order again by using a large machine called a *card sorter*.

To use the machine, you would put cards in a bin, set the machine to sort on the least significant digit (often column 80), and start it. As you waited, the machine would place every card with a zero in column 80 into hopper zero, every card with a one in column 80 into hopper one, and so on. Then you would take the ten decks out, put them together, and run them through again, this time on the second least significant digit. Then the third. And so on.

Each pass through the card sorter would take $O(n)$ time, where n was the number of cards. To sort on d digits required d passes, so the total running time was $O(d \times n)$. For any given card deck, d was a constant number of digits, so $O(d \times n)$ could be regarded as $O(n)$ running time.

Although punched-card sorters are long obsolete, the ideas behind this algorithm can still be used in certain specialized problems.

2.16 BIG-O NOTATION

Big-O notation represents a huge simplification when computing the running time of an algorithm. We eliminate most of the constants. In the case of a polynomial, we eliminate all but the highest term, so $O(n^2 + 3n + 5)$ becomes simply $O(n^2)$. If we are adding terms and one term has a higher degree than the others, we discard the lower degree terms: $O(n^2) + O(n)$ becomes simply $O(n^2)$. Have we *over*simplified things?

For small problems, yes. With Big-O, we assume that small problems run fast enough anyway (usually true, but not always), and it's the large problems that we need to be concerned about.

Key takeaway: Big-O is all about *large* problems.

We can order Big-O times from best to worst:

- O(0) — Zero time. Avoid doing it at all.

- O(1) — Constant time.

- O(log n) — Log time.

- O(n) — Linear time.

- O(n log n) — Log-linear time.

- $O(n^2)$ — Quadratic time.

- $O(n^3)$ — Cubic time.

- $O(n^k)$ — Polynomial time, k > 3.

- $O(2^n)$ — Exponential time.

For large values of n, these represent a range of values almost impossible to express in a single graph. See Figure 2.2 for a comparison of just a few of these running times.

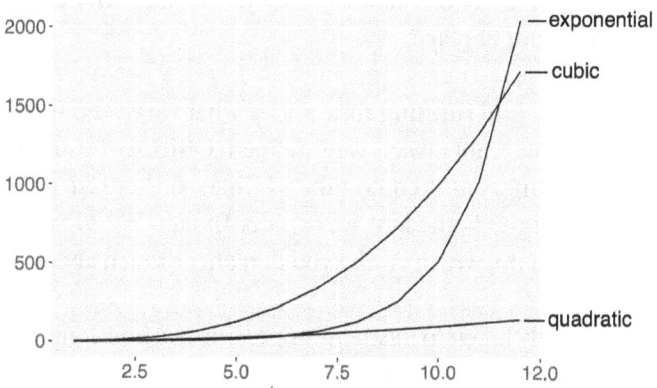

FIGURE 2.2   Comparison of running times.

There are also some algorithms that require **superexponential** time, such as $O(2^{n^c})$. Any such algorithms are beyond the scope of this book.

2.17 BIG-O AND FRIENDS

I said at the beginning of this chapter that it was important to understand Big-O notation. This final section is optional; feel free to skip it if you're tired of analysis, or continue if you want a little deeper understanding.

Along with Big-O, two other measures are sometimes encountered. They are Big-Ω ("big omega") and Big-Θ ("big theta"). Loosely speaking, here's what these measures tell us:

- Big-Ω — The algorithm always takes at least this long.

- Big-Θ — This is how long the algorithm really takes.

- Big-O — The algorithm never takes longer than this.

Big-Ω gives us a *minimum* running time as a function of n, the problem size. This usually isn't very interesting. Some sorting techniques are Big-Ω(n) because they go through the array and find nothing out of place.

Big-Θ is the *actual* running time and is what we would really like to have, but that's not always well-defined. Quicksort usually runs in n log(n) time, but it could take n^2 time, so there isn't a Big-Θ value for it. Big-O is the best we can do. In fact, Big-O is the best we *usually* can do, which is why you don't hear much about Big-Θ.

Big-O is usually taken to mean *the* upper limit on how long an algorithm takes, but it can also be used to mean *an* upper limit. If an algorithm actually takes quadratic time, $O(n^2)$, then it can correctly be described as $O(n^3)$, $O(n^4)$, $O(2^n)$, $O(n \times 2^n)$, and in many other ways. A catch-all term for these longer running times is called **little-o**.

An algorithm has little-o running time if, for sufficiently large n, the algorithm is always faster than this. Put another way, if an algorithm takes O(f(n)) running time and also o(g(n)) running time, then f(n)/g(n) approaches zero as n goes to infinity.

Again, notice that we simply *don't care* what happens for small values of n, but only care about what happens when n is greater than some number N. The precise value of N doesn't matter; only that it exists.

Here are the algorithms we've covered so far:

- Binary search: $\Omega(1)$ (constant time), O(log n).

- Bubble sort: $\Omega(n)$, O(n²).

- Insertion sort: $\Omega(n)$, O(n²).

- Selection sort: $\Omega(n²)$, O(n²), $\Theta(n²)$.

- Quicksort: $\Omega(n \log n)$, O(n²).

- Mergesort: $\Omega(n \log n)$, $\Theta(n \log n)$, O(n log n).

One way to check your understanding of these algorithms and Big-O notation would be to review the algorithms and see if you agree with the above list.

2.18 EXPONENTIAL TIME

Some problems require **exponential time**, and only the smallest of such problems can be solved on conventional computers. (Quantum computing may change this.)

One example is the well-known ***traveling salesman problem***. A salesman wishes to visit a certain number of cities, traveling the minimum possible total distance, and returning to his starting point. If the cities in question are the 48 capitals of the contiguous

United States, there are *47!* (47 factorial) possible paths. If the salesman is limited, at each city, to choosing from five different cities (say, the five nearest ones), there are still about 5^{46} possible paths.

Optimizing is finding the best solution. This may require finding and comparing all solutions, which isn't always possible.

Satisficing is finding a solution that is "good enough." If there is no clear definition of "good enough," then it may be necessary to use the best result found in the time available, whether or not it is satisfactory.

Here's an analogy: If you are about to buy a car, there may be one car out there that is the best choice for you. To find it, you would have to visit every car dealer, compare all the models, compare all the features of each model, and compare their prices and warranties. Nobody can do that. Instead, you *satisfice*: You shop around, get a general idea of what is available, and buy the best car you can find with the time and energy you have available.

For many exponential problems, satisficing is the best you can do.

CHAPTER 3

Hash Tables and Hash Maps I

A FTER ARRAYS, A *HASH map* is probably the most important data structure you will ever need.

Most large programs spend a considerable amount of time looking things up. Hash tables and hash maps are data structures that allow very fast lookup.

A *table* is just a list of values, and looking up something in a table means finding if it is in the table and possibly noting its location. A *map* is a data structure that associates *keys* with values; looking something up means finding the matching key and returning the associated value.

> **Python programmers**: A *dictionary* is basically a hash map.

Whether we are looking up values in a hash table or looking up keys in a hash map, the algorithm is the same. Since a table is slightly simpler than a map, we'll start with tables.

DOI: 10.1201/9781003625506-3

3.1 BASIC HASH TABLES

Consider the problem of searching an unordered array for a given value. Either the value is in the array or it isn't. If it isn't, we need to look at all n elements to determine this. But if the value is in the array, we will find it after looking at n/2 elements, on average. Either way, the search takes linear O(n) time.

If the array is sorted, we can do a binary search. A binary search requires O(log n) time and is about equally fast whether the element is found or not. It doesn't seem like we could do much better—but we can.

Suppose we were to come up with a "magic function" that, given a value to search for, would tell us exactly where in the array to look. If the value is in that location, it's in the array, and if it's not in that location, it's not in the array.

This "magic function" would have no other purpose. If we look at how the function transforms its input to its output, it probably won't make sense (it's magic, after all). This function is called a **hash function** because it "makes hash" of its inputs.

We can't actually do magic, but we can come close. We'll demonstrate with an extremely small but otherwise reasonable example.

Suppose you are a bird watcher and want to keep a table of all the birds you have seen. You can look in the table to determine if you've seen a particular kind of bird, and you can add new birds to the table. We'll use an array of ten elements (absurdly small, but big enough for an example). For a hash function, we'll use the number of characters in the bird's name.

> **Remember**: Since strings vary in length, an "array of strings" is really an array of *pointers* to strings.

So far, you've seen a wren, a cardinal, a robin, and a chickadee, and your hash table looks like the table on the right of Figure 3.1.

```
hashCode("wren") = 4
hashCode("cardinal") = 8
hashCode("robin") = 5
hashCode("chickadee") = 9
```

0	
1	
2	
3	
4	wren
5	robin
6	
7	
8	cardinal
9	chickadee

FIGURE 3.1   Hash table.

With this table, you can tell you have seen a robin by computing hashCode("robin") = 5 and finding "robin" at location 5 of the table. You haven't seen a sparrow, because hashCode("sparrow") is 7, and location 7 of the hash table is empty.

Suppose you next see a hummingbird and want to add it to the table. Unfortunately, "hummingbird" is 11 characters long, and there are only ten locations in our table. The solution, regardless of what hash function is used, is to always take the result *mod the table size*.

> **Reminder:** *Mod* (short for "*modulo*") is the remainder of an integer division. For example, *14 mod 5* is 4, since 5 goes into 14 twice with 4 left over. In many languages the symbol % denotes this "mod" operation.

> **Note:** Our example assumes 0-based arrays. If your language uses 1-based arrays, use (i-1) % n + 1 instead of i % n, where i is the index and n is the table size.

Since hashCode("hummingbird") % 10 = 1, "hummingbird" goes into location 1 of the table; see Figure 3.2.

```
hashCode("wren") = 4
hashCode("cardinal") = 8
hashCode("robin") = 5
hashCode("chickadee") = 9
hashCode("hummingbird") = 1
```

0	
1	hummingbird
2	
3	
4	wren
5	robin
6	
7	
8	cardinal
9	chickadee

FIGURE 3.2   Modified hash table.

A more serious problem occurs when we spot a crow, hash-Code("crow") % 10 = 4. (It's easier to always take the mod rather than first checking whether we need to.) Location 4 already contains the word wren. This is called a **collision**.

When a collision occurs, one solution is to **probe** (look at) the next location, and the next, and the next, until we find an empty location. In our "crow" example, we see that location 4 is already occupied (and not by "crow"), so we look at location 5 and see that it is already occupied (and not by "crow"), so we look at location 6 and it's empty, so we can put "crow" in location 6.

If we had found a location with "crow" in it, we would know that "crow" was already in the table, and we could stop there.

If instead of trying to add "crow" to the table, we simply wanted to know if it was already there, we would follow the same procedure. We would probe location 4 ("wren"), location 5 ("robin"), and location 6 (empty). Since we find an empty location before finding "crow," it follows that "crow" is not in the table.

3.2 HASH FUNCTIONS

Properly implemented, looking something up in a hash table or putting something into a hash table will take only O(1) constant time. This is an impressive claim; can we justify it?

The full math is beyond this book, but we can approach it. Let's start with two assumptions. (1) Our hash function is really good, so different inputs almost always produce different outputs. (2) Our table is really big, so collisions are highly unlikely. In these circumstances, it should be obvious that most searches take constant time, at the cost of a great deal of wasted space.

Let's look at the hash function first.

- The hash function must be deterministic—given the same input, it will always produce the same result. This means it can't use random numbers, the time of day, or anything like that.

- The hash function should be fast to compute. After all, the goal is speedy lookup.

- The hash function should give a wide range of values (ideally, any 32- or 64-bit positive integer).

- The hash function should give very different results for even tiny changes in the input.

Let's look at the hash function in our example: the length of a bird's name. It will always produce the same result for the same bird's name (required); counting letters is reasonably fast (good); it gives a very small range of values (even the longest name is probably only a couple of dozen characters (bad)); and names like "catbird" and "cowbird" have the same hash code (bad). All in all, not a very good hash function.

Your programming language probably provides much better hash functions for common objects. For a string s, Java uses:

```
s[0]*31^(n-1) + s[1]*31^(n-2) + ... + s[n-1]
```

where s[i] is the ith character of the string, n is the length of the string, and ^ indicates exponentiation. (Exponentiation to a power of 2 is a fast operation, as it is simply a bit shift.)

The size of the hash table also matters. Obviously, we don't want it to get too full. The more the hash table contains, the more collisions will occur. The more collisions occur, the slower it will be to look something up or to insert something. A good rule of thumb is to make the table large enough so that it never gets more than about 70% full. At this size, we can typically find the correct location with only two or three probes. (Some individual searches might take quite a bit longer, but *on average* we can expect constant time.)

We might create a hash table with 1000 entries—a nice round number. Surprisingly, a nice round number is a poor choice for the size of a hash table. Here's why:

Suppose *f* is a factor of the table size *t*, that is, *t=f x* for some integer *x*. We find a hash code *h* for the value we want to put in the table and compute *h* mod *t* (*h* % *t*) to decide where to insert it. Unfortunately, if *h* has *f* as a factor, then *h* % *t* will also have *f* as a factor. There are only a limited number of table locations that are multiples of *f*, therefore collisions are more likely.

Consequently, we prefer a table size that has as few factors as possible. A prime number has the fewest number of factors, namely, itself and 1. Therefore, we should choose a *prime number* close to the size we want—say, 997 or 1009, rather than 1000.

3.3 HASH TABLE NOTES

When values are added to a hash table, the first entries receive the best locations. As the table fills up, later entries encounter more collisions. This means that when entering values from a "natural" source, such as words from English text (or the birds in your backyard), the values needed most often will be the fastest to look up.

Hash tables should be created with enough space so that they don't become too full—preferably not more than about 70%. However, even up to about 95%, hash tables are still quite efficient. When a hash table becomes too full, the usual solution is to allocate space for a larger table and rehash everything.

It is not usually possible to delete an item from a hash table. If this must be done, one approach is to leave the item in the table but somehow mark it as not available. Another approach is to remove all the values in the surrounding "clump" and then reinsert all but the unwanted value. A third approach is to use a linked hash table (see Section 6.8).

3.4 HASH MAPS

A *hash map* is a simple extension of a hash table. Associated with each entry in the map is some data about that entry, often in the form of a link.

There are two simple ways to implement such a hash map. First, it can be done with an array of objects, where each object has a string field to contain the name of a bird, and a pointer to information about that bird. See Figure 3.3.

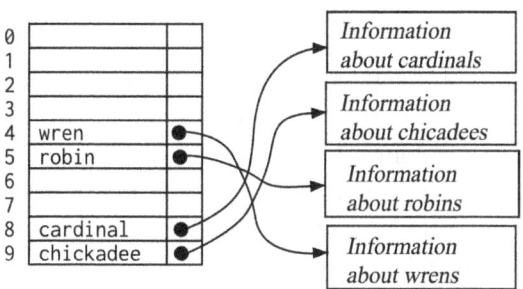

FIGURE 3.3   Hash map.

The second implementation is to use two arrays: one for bird names and the other for bird information. The bird name can be looked up in the first array, and the same index can be used to access information in the second array.

3.5 ABSTRACT DATA TYPES

A *data type* is characterized by (1) a set of **values**, such as {..., -2, -1, 0, 1, 2,...}, or {true, false}; (2) a data **representation**, which is common to all these values E; and (3) a set of **operations**, which can be applied uniformly to all these values.

To *abstract* is to leave out unnecessary information. In an *abstract data type* (*ADT*), the data representation is abstracted away; only the values and operations are provided.

For example, suppose you define a "lookup table" in which a user can (1) create a new lookup table, (2) add an item to the table, and (3) test if an item is in the table. Then you hide the implementation (by making the array "private," or however you hide code in your language), so that no other access to the lookup table is allowed. You have an ADT.

Hiding the implementation is important for two main reasons. First, it allows you to modify the implementation as needed. Second, it helps localize errors.

You might implement a lookup table as a sorted array and use a binary search to insert or look up values. If you didn't hide the implementation, someone who wants the smallest value in the lookup table might simply get the first element of the array. This code will break if you change the implementation from a sorted array to a hash table.

The primary user of your lookup table is probably yourself. If you need to get the smallest value in the table, you can add a new operation to do this. Then, if you change the implementation, you just need to recode this operation along with all the others.

Errors happen. If some error puts your lookup table in an inconsistent state, and the only access to the implementation is through methods you provide, then the error is in your methods. But if the implementation is exposed, then any code anywhere in the program could be causing the problem (and you bear the blame).

> **Moral:** Data structures should always be implemented as abstract data types.

One of the benefits of object-oriented languages is the ability to treat a data structure as an "object," with a hidden implementation and a limited set of operations on that object.

3.5.1 ADT as a Contract

Every ADT should have a ***contract*** (or ***specification***) that tells the users everything they need to know in order to use the ADT, and does *not* tell the user anything they do not need to know. In particular, they do not need to know your data representation or your algorithms.

A contract is an agreement between two parties. In this case, one party is the implementer of the ADT, who is concerned with making the operations correct and efficient, and the other party is the applications programmer, who just wants to use the ADT to get a job done. It doesn't matter if you are both of these parties; the contract is still helpful for good code and is critical in any large project.

What makes a good contract? If you buy a house, you want to pay as little as possible. If you sell a house, you want to get as much as possible. You want a contract that is in your favor.

The same principle applies when designing an ADT. You will almost always be in a position where you know what the ADT will be used for, and you should provide that much functionality *and no more.* This keeps down both the cost and the complexity of your ADT. Of course, it's nice if the design is such that more functionality *can* be added later, when it may be needed, but it's generally a mistake to write code before it is actually needed.

When designing an ADT, keep efficiency in mind and use an implementation that reduces the Big-O running time of the most frequently used operations.

Your ADT should be documented. Just do it! Programmers are notoriously bad at getting around to documenting code, so here is an area where it's easy to excel.

If the documentation is too hard to write, this probably means the ADT is too hard to use. In that case, it's the ADT that should be fixed.

If you design for generality, it's easy to add functionality later—but you can't remove functionality unless you are absolutely sure that it has never been used.

CHAPTER 4

Recursion

A **RECURSIVE DEFINITION** IS A definition in which the thing being defined occurs as part of its own definition. Many data structures are defined recursively; for example, a list may contain sublists. Functions can call themselves to solve simpler subproblems. We will see many examples of both.

This chapter exists because recursion is frequently (and unfortunately) considered an "advanced" topic. It shouldn't be. Recursive code is no harder to understand than loops and is often easier. Moreover, recursion is essential for working with many data structures.

If you are comfortable with recursion, feel free to skip this chapter. There's nothing in it specifically about data structures, so you won't miss anything.

4.1 RECURSIVE DATA STRUCTURES

A **natural number** can be defined recursively:

- 1, or

- Any natural number plus 1.

DOI: 10.1201/9781003625506-4

So 1 is a natural number because of rule one; 2 is a natural number because it is the natural number 1 plus 1; 3 is a natural number because it is the natural number 2 plus 1; and so on.

As a more practical example, a *list* is:

- An open parenthesis,
- Zero or more numbers or lists, and
- A close parenthesis.

By this definition, (), (1 2 17), and ((1) (1 2) (1 2 3)) are all lists.

Indirect recursion occurs when a thing is defined in terms of other things, but those other things are defined in terms of the first thing. For example,

An *arithmetic expression* is any of:

- A number,
- A *sum*, *product*, *difference*, or *quotient*, or
- Parentheses around an arithmetic expression.

A *sum* is:

- An arithmetic expression,
- A plus sign, and
- An arithmetic expression.

... and similarly for *product*, *difference*, and *quotient*. We've left out a few operations, but the above is sufficient to express (1 + 2) * (3 + 4 + 5).

Recursion is a common characteristic of nested structures such as lists, arithmetic expressions, and computer programs (statements within statements). We'll see many examples of these.

4.2 RECURSIVE FUNCTIONS

Functions (or "methods," if you prefer) can also be recursive. A *recursive function* is one that calls itself. Every modern programming language allows recursive functions, and they are extremely useful for working with recursive data structures.

When a function is entered, it gets a *new* set of local variables. In a recursive function, these have the same *names* as in other levels of the recursion, but they occupy different storage locations and therefore can have different values. This makes it possible to change a local variable at one level of recursion without affecting those variables with the same name at other levels.

Parameters passed by value are effectively local variables.

The (inevitable) first example of a recursive function is the factorial.

The factorial of a natural number n is the product of all the natural numbers up to and including n. For example, the factorial of 5 (written $5!$) is the result of $1 \times 2 \times 3 \times 4 \times 5$. From this, it's easy to see that 5! can be computed by multiplying 4! by 5, that is, $(1 \times 2 \times 3 \times 4) \times 5$.

Since the factorial of 1 is simply 1, we can write the factorial function as

```
function factorial(n):
    If n == 1, return 1,
    else return factorial(n - 1) * n.
```

Here, the n == 1 case is a ***base case***: a case that can be computed without recursion. Every recursive function must have at least one base case.

The advantage of using the factorial to demonstrate recursion is that it is easy to understand; the disadvantage is that using a loop is arguably simpler and certainly much more efficient. This isn't a great use of recursion.

Here's a somewhat better example. Suppose you want to ask the user a yes–no question but don't trust the user to respond sensibly.

```
function askYesOrNo(question):
    Display the question.
    Read in the answer.
    If answer starts with "Y" or "y", return TRUE.
    If answer starts with "N" or "n", return FALSE.
    Display "Please answer with 'yes' or 'no'.".
    Call askYesOrNo(question) and return the result.
```

If the user responds with, say, Maybe, this code just calls itself again, and the answer returned is then returned from the original call. It works for any sequence of unacceptable answers, not just one. You can do the same thing without recursion, but it takes a little extra work.

4.3 FOUR RULES

There are four rules that are very helpful in writing recursive functions, particularly if you are just learning to use recursion.

1. Do the base cases first.

2. Recur only with simpler cases.

3. Don't use non-local variables.

4. Don't look down.

4.3.1 Rule 1: Do Base Cases First

Every valid recursive definition consists of two parts:

- One or more **base cases**, where you compute the answer directly, without recursion; and

- One or more **recursive cases**, where you do *part* of the work and recur with a simpler problem.

Every recursive function *must* have base cases. If your function accidentally recurs with what should have been a base case, it's likely to result in an infinite recursion. Checking for and handling base cases before doing any recursions, although not absolutely necessary, makes this problem less likely.

The following definition of the factorial function works equally well for natural numbers.

```
function factorial(n):
    If n > 1, return factorial(n - 1) * n,
    else return 1.
```

This version does not explicitly list n==1 as a base case and, in fact, it behaves differently for zero and negative numbers.

4.3.2 Rule 2: Recur Only with Simpler Cases

If the problem isn't simple enough to be a base case, break it into two parts:

- A *simpler* problem or problems of the same kind, and

- *Extra work* to use the solution of the simpler problem to solve the given problem.

The factorial function clearly does this. The simpler problem is finding the factorial of a smaller number (a number closer to 1), and the extra work is multiplying by n.

"Simpler" means "more like a base case." It can involve using a smaller number, a smaller part of a data structure, or just about anything.

Any time you recur with a case that isn't closer to a base case, you get the recursive equivalent of an infinite loop.

```
function factorial(n):
    If n == 1, return 1,
    else return factorial(n).
```

4.3.3 Rule 3: Don't Use Non-Local Variables

Ideally, a function should use its parameters, and only its parameters, to compute a result. This makes the function more self-contained and therefore easier to understand and debug.

A *global* variable is one that is accessible to all parts of the program. It doesn't (typically) get copied, so any change to it is visible everywhere in the program.

If a parameter is passed *by reference*, this means that there is only one copy of that value, and what the function receives is a link or pointer to that value. Therefore, a reference parameter behaves like a global variable.

It's acceptable for a recursive function to refer to a global variable, as long as it doesn't also change it. For example, a recursive function can look up values in a dictionary or a hash table.

It's also acceptable for a recursive function to modify a global variable if that variable isn't used in the computation. For example, a recursive function might use a global variable to count the number of times an operation is performed.

The problem arises when we try to *both* modify a global variable *and* use it in the recursion. This usually isn't a problem with simple numerical calculations, but can get complicated when a data structure is involved.

4.3.4 Rule 4: Don't Look Down

Some texts have suggested that the way to understand a recursive function is to examine how it works at all levels of recursion. This may be a good way to convince yourself that recursion *can* work, but it's not a good way to try to understand or debug a particular recursive function. It's hard enough to understand *one level* of *one function* at a time; it's almost impossible to keep track of many levels of the same function all at once. Don't even try!

If you try to understand a non-recursive function that happens to call other functions, you do not immediately start examining those other functions to see how they work. Instead, you begin by assuming that those other functions are correct.

The same should hold for recursive functions. In order to understand a recursive function, you should assume the recursive calls are doing the correct thing. If there is an error in them, then that same error occurs at *this* level, where you can find it. If you can get *this* level correct, you will automatically get *all* levels correct.

There is never any need to "look down" into a recursion.

4.4 EXAMPLES OF RECURSION

We'll briefly consider three examples. First is our old friend, the factorial.

```
function factorial(n):
    If n == 1, return 1,
    else return factorial(n - 1) * n.
```

We ask the following questions:

- Did we cover all possible cases?

    - If n is a natural number (a positive integer), then n is either 1 or larger than 1, so we have covered all cases.

    - If n is not a natural number (0, negative, or a real number), then there are cases for which the function may not (and does not) work.

- Did we recur only with simpler cases?

    - The "simplest" case is 1, and every recursive call is with a number that is closer to 1, so yes.

- Did we change any non-local variables?

    - No.

Therefore, the function is probably correct.

For a second example, let's try to make factorial more efficient by performing two multiplications at each level.

```
function factorial(n):
    If n == 1, return 1,
    else return factorial(n - 2) * (n - 1) * n.
```

We'll ask the same questions again.

- Did we cover all possible cases?

    - If n is a natural number (a positive integer), then n is either 1 or larger than 1, so we have covered all cases.

    - As before, n must be a natural number.

- Did we recur only with simpler cases?

    - Is every recursive call with a number closer to 1? No, because 1 is odd, and if we start with an even number, we'll recur only with even numbers, and overshoot 1.

Finally, we'll look at the *Fibonacci series*. This is a sequence of natural numbers starting with 1, 1. Each subsequent number is the sum of the two previous numbers, giving 1, 1, 2, 3, 5, 8, 13, 21, and so on. The n-th Fibonacci number is easy to compute with a loop.

The first and second Fibonacci numbers are both 1. The definition of the n-th Fibonacci number, for n > 2, is

```
fibonacci(n) = fibonacci(n - 1) + fibonacci(n - 2)
```

and this is also easy to compute with two recursions.

```
function fibonacci(n):
    If n < 3, return 1
    else return fibonacci(n - 1) + fibonacci(n - 2).
```

While easy (and correct), this is not efficient. Since there are two recursions at each level, the number of calls increases exponentially. For n = 10, only 109 calls are required, but for n = 30, 1664079 calls are required. For an efficient solution, see Section 13.5.

CHAPTER 5

Stacks, Queues, and Deques

S TACKS, QUEUES, AND DEQUES are similar data structures. They consist of a linear sequence of values, to which new values can be added at an end or removed from an end.

- In a stack, insertions and deletions are performed at the same end.

- In a queue, insertions are performed at one end and deletions at the other end.

- In a deque, insertions and deletions can be performed at either end.

5.1 STACKS

A *stack* is an abstract data type with the following operations:

- **Create** a new, empty stack.

- **Test** if a stack is empty.

 DOI: 10.1201/9781003625506-5

- **Push** a new value onto the stack.

- **Peek** at the "top" (most recently added) element of a stack. Return it but do not remove it.

- **Pop** (remove) the "top" element of a stack and return it.

Other operations may be added as needed, for example, returning the number of elements on the stack or testing if an element occurs within the stack, but the above operations are fundamental.

Items are inserted at one end of a stack and removed from the same end. The consequence is that items will be removed in the reverse order from that in which they were added. For this reason, a stack is sometimes called a *LIFO* (last in, first out) data structure.

A stack can be implemented with two components: one array and one integer. See Figure 5.1.

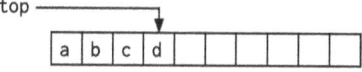

FIGURE 5.1   Array implementation of a stack.

In Figure 5.1, the values a, b, c, and d, in that order, have been pushed onto the stack. The most recently pushed value, d, is at the top of the stack; the next item that is pushed will be added after it.

The integer top can be defined in several ways. It can be the index of the topmost element (as in Figure 5.1), the index of the first available location (just past d), or as a count of how many items are in the stack.

With this implementation, two errors can occur: *overflow*, in which the number of items added exceeds the size of the array, and **underflow**, when an attempt is made to peek or pop from an empty stack. In Section 6.2, we will see an implementation that allows stacks of virtually unlimited size.

All stack operations, except possibly creation, take O(1) time.

5.1.1 Example: Balancing Brackets

A simple use of stacks is to determine whether "brackets" (in the general sense, including parentheses, braces, HTML tags, or others) are balanced—that is, every open bracket has a matching close bracket.

Omitting all the enclosed content, we can determine that ([]({()} [()])) is balanced; ([]({()}[()])) is not.

Simple counting is not enough to check balance, but you can do it with a stack. Going from left to right:

- If you see a (, [, or {, push it onto the stack.

- If you see a),], or }, pop the stack and check whether you got the corresponding (, [, or {; if not, it's an error.

- When you reach the end, check that the stack is empty.

5.1.2 Example: Expression Evaluation

You can evaluate an expression, such as 1+2*3+4, using two stacks: one for operands (numbers) and the other for operators.

The basic algorithm is as follows. Proceeding from left to right:

- If you see a number, push it onto the number stack.

- If you see an operator,

    - **While** the top of the operator stack holds an operator of equal or higher precedence:

- Pop the old operator,

- Pop the top two values from the number stack and apply the old operator to them, and

- Push the result onto the number stack,

- Push the new operator onto the operator stack.

- At the end, perform any remaining operations.

There are several elaborations that can be made.

If a unary minus is encountered, push a zero onto the operand stack and proceed as you would for a subtraction operator. (A minus is a unary operator if it is the first thing in an expression, if it immediately follows an open parenthesis, or if it immediately follows another operator.)

An opening parenthesis can be treated as a low-priority operator that does nothing. When a right parenthesis is encountered, perform all the operations on the operator stack up to the left parenthesis, then remove the left parenthesis from the operator stack.

The operator stack will occasionally become empty. To avoid treating this as a special case, invent a new "operator" with the lowest possible priority and initialize the operator stack with this value. To apply this operator, just quit, because all the work has been done.

Table 5.1 shows the evaluation of 2*(3+4), using '_' as the "quit" operator.

5.1.3 Example: Stack Frames

All modern programming languages use a stack to keep track of function calls and local variables.

TABLE 5.1   Evaluating 2*(3+4)

Scanned Value	Operator Stack	Operand Stack
2	['_']	[2]
*	['_', '*']	[2]
(	['_', '*', '(']	[2]
3	['_', '*', '(']	[2, 3]
+	['_', '*', '(', '+']	[2, 3]
4	['_', '*', '(', '+']	[2, 3, 4]
)	['_', '*']	[2, 7]
	['_']	[14]

Functions can call other functions and can be recursive (they can call themselves). At each call, the location of the calling statement (the **return address**) is pushed onto a **call stack**. If no errors interrupt the process, each return from a function pops a value from the call stack, and execution returns to that popped location.

Each function has its own set of local variables, including its parameters. Storage for these variables is allocated when the function is called and released when the function returns. These local variables are also pushed onto the call stack when the function is entered and popped off when the function returns.

If all the local variables can be determined at compile time, they can be put into a node called a **stack frame**. This single entity can then, along with the return address, be pushed onto and popped off from the stack.

5.2 QUEUES

A **queue** is an abstract data type with the following operations:

- **Create** a new, empty queue.

- **Test** if a queue is empty.

- **Enqueue** (add) a new value onto the "rear" of the queue.

- **Peek** at the element at the "front" of the queue. Return it but do not remove it.

- **Dequeue** (remove) the "front" element of a queue and return it.

Other operations may be added as needed; the above operations are fundamental.

Queues implement a "first come, first served" strategy. Items are inserted at one end of the queue and removed from the opposite end, similar to a checkout line in a store. Queues are sometimes called *FIFO* (first in, first out) data structures.

A queue can be implemented with three components: one array and two integers. Figure 5.2 shows what a queue would look like after the items a through g have been added to it and items a through c have been removed.

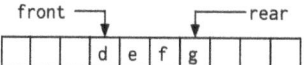

FIGURE 5.2   Array implementation of a queue.

To enqueue (add) an element, the rear index must be incremented, and to dequeue (remove) an element, the front index must be incremented. As a result, the array contents "creep forward." To deal with this, incrementation is done modulo the array size, so that the array is effectively circular—the first element immediately follows the last element.

> **Note:** If your language uses 1-based arrays, use (i-1) % n + 1 instead of i % n, where i is the index and n is the table size.

When the queue has exactly one element, front and rear will be equal. When the queue is empty, rear will be equal to front-1 (modulo the array size). When every queue location holds a value, rear will also be equal to front-1! This means an empty queue cannot be distinguished from a full queue. Obviously, this is a problem.

Here are three solutions.:

- Make the array large enough so that it never gets full. This works (for a while) but is a disaster waiting to happen. Please don't do this.

- Declare the queue to be full when rear equals front-2 (modulo the array size), so that one array location remains unused. Any attempt to enqueue something more will result in an **overflow error**.

- Keep a count of the number of elements in the queue, and don't let it exceed the array size. This also works, but it requires a bit more work and has no obvious advantages.

An attempt to dequeue something from an empty queue will result in an **underflow error**.

All queue operations, except possibly creation, take O(1) time.

5.3 DEQUES

A *deque* (pronounced "deck") is an abstract data type. The operations are the same as those of a queue, except that insertions and deletions (and peeks) may be performed at either end.

Deques are rarely used and the names of the operations vary considerably from one implementation to another. We might, for example, have add_left and add_right to enqueue items, or perhaps add_at_front and add_at_rear.

A deque, like a queue, can be implemented with an array and two integer indices. Like a queue, deque operations take O(1) time.

CHAPTER 6

Linked Lists

M OST LANGUAGES PROVIDE ONE or more data structures called "lists." *Don't be misled by names!* Any data structure that represents a sequence of values can be called a list. In Python, for example, a "list" is implemented as an array.

In many languages, a "list" is a structure built around one of the two types of *basic* lists that we will explore in this chapter: the singly linked list (SLL) and the doubly linked list (DLL).

6.1 SINGLY LINKED LISTS

An singly linked list (***SLL***) can be implemented as an abstract data type with the following operations:

- is_empty(***list***) — Test if the list is empty (has no elements).

- head(***list***) — Return the first element of the list.

- tail(***list***) — Return the portion of the list containing everything after the first element.

- cons(***value***, ***list***) — Return the list with the value added as a new first element.

DOI: 10.1201/9781003625506-6

The names of the operations may vary, but head, tail, and cons ("construct") are commonly used. Surprisingly, these four operations are all that are commonly needed.

Singly linked lists are implemented as a collection of nodes, where each node contains a **value** field and a **next** field. The value field can hold whatever data the programmer chooses, while the next field holds a pointer to the next node in the sequence. The next field of the last node in the list is a "null" pointer, one that doesn't point to anything. Depending on your language, a null pointer could be null (Java), None (Python), the number 0 (C), or something similar.

Figure 6.1 represents a singly linked lists containing the values a, b, c, and d. Links are represented by solid circles and arrows, while the slash represents a "null link."

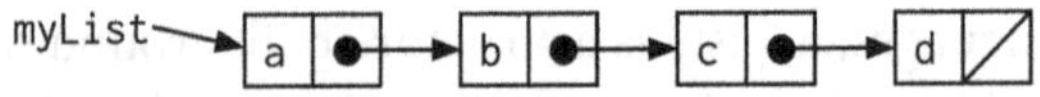

FIGURE 6.1   A singly linked list.

To create a non-empty list, the simplest way to begin is to cons a value onto the empty list. Then cons a value onto that, and then another, building the list in reverse order. For example, Figure 6.1 could be created using the following code.

```
myList = cons(a, cons(b, cons(c, cons(d, NULL))))
```

In this example, head(myList) is the value a, and tail(myList) is the list b, c, d. Also notice that head(tail(myList)) is the value b, and tail(tail(myList)) is the list c, d.

Recursive functions and singly linked lists are ideally suited for each other. To write a recursive function on a list, the fundamental recipe is: *Do something with the head and recur with the tail.* For example, to find the length of a list:

```
function length(L):
if L is empty, return 0
else return 1 + length(tail(L))
```

To find the sum of elements in a numerical list:

```
function sum(L):
    if L is empty, return 0
    else return head(L) + sum(tail(L))
```

To get the last element in a *non-empty* list:

```
function last(L):
    if tail(L) is empty, return head(L)
    else return last(tail(L))
```

To get the largest element in a *non-empty* numerical list:

```
function largest(L):
    if tail(L) is empty, return head(L)
    else:
        tail_max = largest(tail(L))
        if head(L) > tail_max, return head(L)
        else return tail_max
```

To reverse a stack, the simplest algorithm is to create a second, empty stack, and then successively move all the elements from the first stack onto the second stack.

```
function reverse(L, L2):
    if L is empty, return L2
    return reverse(tail(L), cons(head(L, L2)))
```

To use reverse, the user must remember to create a second, empty stack and pass it in as the L2 parameter. This isn't ideal. In cases like this, it's better to provide a *façade function*—another function that "stands in front of" the function that does the work, and whose only purpose is to provide a nicer interface.

```
function reverse(L):
    return help_reverse(L, empty list)

function help_reverse(L, L2):
    if L is empty, return L2
    return help_reverse(tail(L), cons(head(L, L2)))
```

The operations is_empty, head, and tail all take O(1) time. The cons operator allocates memory for a new node, which we can assume also takes O(1) time.

6.2 STACKS AS SINGLY LINKED LISTS

As noted earlier, a stack can be viewed as an abstract data type with the following operations: **Create** a new, empty stack; **Test** if a stack is empty; **Push** a new value onto the stack; **Peek** at the "top" of a stack; and **Pop** (remove and return) the "top" element of a stack.

A stack can be implemented directly with a singly linked list (see Figure 6.2).

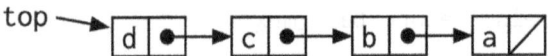

FIGURE 6.2   Stack as a linked list.

The operations on a stack are almost exactly the same as the operations on a linked list.

- To create a stack, create a singly linked list.

- To test if a stack is empty, test if the list is empty.

- To push a value onto a stack, cons it onto the list, then set the pointer to the front of the list to the node containing this new value. That is, *list* = cons(*value*, *list*).

- To peek at a stack, return the head of the list.

- To pop a stack, get and hold the head. Then set the pointer to the list to the tail of the list. Return the held value. That is, *value* = head(*list*); *list* = tail(*list*); return *value*.

One advantage of this implementation over using an array is that stack *overflow* never happens. (You can run out of available memory, but that's a somewhat different problem.) Another advantage is that if you already have singly linked lists available, implementing stacks is trivial.

6.3 IMPLEMENTATION NOTES

The easiest way to create an singly linked list is to define a node type with head and tail fields, where the head holds a data value and the tail holds a pointer to the next node in the sequence. Then, it's easy to define head(*node*), tail(*node*), cons(*value*, *node*), and other functions.

In an object-oriented language, however, it's generally desirable to define the methods on an object within the definition of the object. Consequently, you would write *node*.head(), *node*.tail(), and so on. With a more "public" implementation, you might be able to write just *node*.head and *tail*.head, but other methods would still need to be written as method calls, for example, *node*.cons(*value*).

In an object-oriented implementation of lists, empty lists cause some difficulties. If an empty list is represented by a null value, it's not possible to write a *list*.is_empty() function, because you can't call methods on a null value. Instead, to ask if a list is empty, you have to explicitly ask whether *list* equals the null value. To avoid this problem, every list might begin with a special *header node*.

The use of a header node makes it easy to implement the is_empty method and allows the creation of an "empty" list that is distinguishable from a null value. The disadvantage is that every use of the tail operation involves creating a new header node.

A "node," like an "array," is not a specific type, but rather a general designation for a class of types. You can have one kind of node for the elements of singly linked list, another kind for the nodes in a binary tree, and so on. In languages with *strict typing*, the type of every field in a node must be specified in advance. In particular, the type of every *link* must be specified in advance so that when the link is followed, the type of the node it references is known.

In languages with strict typing, it is still possible to have a linked list containing mixed types. The node will have multiple fields, one for each type needed, with an additional flag field to specify which field to use. In Figure 6.3, the first field indicates which of the other fields to use; unused fields are shown in gray.

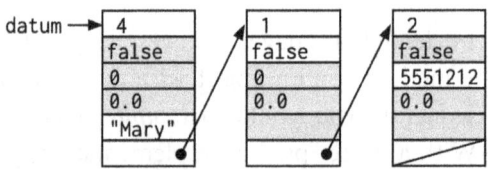

FIGURE 6.3 List with mixed types.

In some applications, lists may have *sublists*—the values in a list may themselves be lists. In any reasonable application, there must be more than just lists of sublists of sublists of sublists; the list must include some actual data at some point. To make this possible, the nodes must have separate fields for the (possible) data and the (possible) link.

A few languages have **variant records** or **tagged unions**. These are nodes containing a tag to specify which type of data is included so that the same memory may be used for different types.

6.4 LISTS IN FUNCTIONAL PROGRAMMING

More and more languages are adding functional programming features, and singly linked lists are an important part of that.

One of the tenets of functional programming is that the value of a variable never changes; instead, new values are saved in new variables. Two tools make this feasible: recursion, in which new local variables are created by recursive calls, and singly linked lists, in which the cons and tail operations return new lists without altering the original list.

Figure 6.4 shows myList from a previous section. List2 is created by consing aa onto myList, and List3 is created by taking the tail of myList. Because pointers are "one way," all this is "invisible" from the viewpoint of myList.

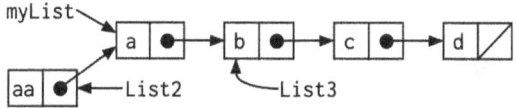

FIGURE 6.4   Three separate lists with shared storage.

The operations defined for singly linked lists in Section 6.1 do not support any changes to the content of lists once they are created, which is perfect for functional programming languages. If such operations are provided, as they might be in a non-functional language, the type of **structure sharing** shown in Figure 6.4 is highly inadvisable.

6.5 DOUBLY LINKED LISTS

A doubly linked list (DLL) can be implemented as a collection of nodes. Each node contains a value, a link to its successor (if any), and a link to its predecessor (if any).

In Figure 6.5, the middle node (containing b) has a previous field pointing to the node containing a and a next field pointing to the node containing c.

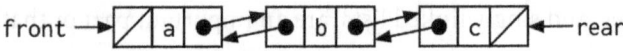

front → a • → • b • → • c ← rear

FIGURE 6.5 A doubly linked list.

As an abstract data type, the operations on a DLL might be called is_empty, front, rear, next, previous, add_to_front, and add_to_rear.

To refer to the list as a whole, you could define a header node with just the fields front and rear. The header points to the first and last nodes in the list (or contains null links if the list is empty).

Doubly linked lists can be useful in applications where it is necessary to traverse the list in either direction.

Operations that manipulate a list, such as inserting nodes at a particular location or deleting nodes, are easier on a list that has links in both directions.

6.6 CIRCULAR LINKED LISTS

Doubly linked lists can be made *circular* so that the link in the last element, rather than being null, points back to the first element. When this is done, "first" and "last" cease to have meaning; given a link to any node in the list, you can go around and around the list in either the forward or backward direction, indefinitely.

Singly linked lists can also be made circular, but doing this loses the advantage of structure sharing (see Section 6.4).

6.7 PYTHON "LISTS"

In Python, a "list" is implemented as an array of pointers, along with two additional values: the number of locations allocated to the array (its *capacity*) and the number actually in use (its *length*).

The values in an array must be all the same type. The values in a Python list may be of varying types and sizes because the array contains only pointers, which are all of the same size.

Indexing into an array takes constant time, and dereferencing a pointer also takes constant time, so accessing an element by its array index takes constant time.

If the array has unused capacity, appending a new item to the end or removing one takes constant time.

If appending a new item exceeds the capacity, then space must be allocated for a new, larger array, and all the values in the array must be copied to the new array. This, of course, takes 0(n) time; however, the new array is chosen to be large enough that adding enough new values will amortize (average out) so that the result will still be 0(1).

A variable whose value is the array cannot simply be a pointer to the storage for that array, since the array may be moved in memory. Instead, such variables must be a *handle* (a pointer to a pointer) to the array. This way, when the array is moved, only a single pointer, in a fixed location, needs to be updated.

For example, suppose a Python list (an array of pointers) needs to be expanded. The list may be referenced by multiple variables (call them ref1, ref2, and ref3), making it difficult to find and change them all. Instead, the following steps are taken (see Figure 6.6):

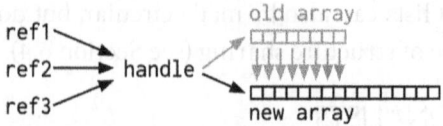

FIGURE 6.6   Relocating an array using a handle.

1. A larger block of storage is allocated.

2. All values are copied from the old storage block to the new storage block.

3. The handle is changed to refer to the new storage block. This makes the old storage block available for garbage collection.

In Figure 6.6, the gray arrow indicates the original pointer from the handle, and the black arrow indicates the new pointer. Note that the variables ref1, ref2, and ref3 remain unchanged.

6.8 HASH TABLES AND HASH MAPS II

The problem of collisions in a hash table can be sidestepped by making each entry in the hash table a pointer to a *list* of entries. See Figure 6.7.

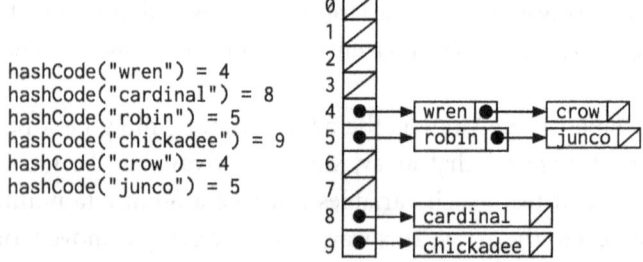

FIGURE 6.7   A hash map using linked lists.

This approach means that a hash table never gets "full"—new entries can always be added (at least until memory is exhausted, but that's a different problem).

When adding to a hash table, we must first check that the item isn't already present. This requires stepping through all the items with the same hash code. If the word being added is dove, this would end at the node containing crow, so it costs about the same to add dove before wren or after crow. In many cases, more frequent items are seen and added earlier, making it desirable to add later, less common entries at the end.

To delete a node from a list, change the pointer of the previous node to point to the node after the one being deleted. That is, if node A points to node B and node B points to node C, you can delete node B by simply changing node A to point to node C. The memory used by B can then be deallocated or garbage collected.

A hash *map* is a hash table in which each entry has associated information. This can be achieved by adding a field to each node. See Figure 6.8 for a small portion of such a hash map.

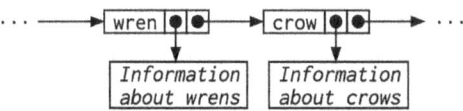

FIGURE 6.8   A hash map using linked lists.

CHAPTER 7

Binary Trees

A **BINARY TREE** IS COMPOSED of zero or more nodes. Each node contains three components: a value (some sort of data item), a reference or pointer to a **left child** (which may be null), and a reference or pointer to a **right child** (which may be null). The children of a node are themselves binary trees.

A binary tree may be empty (contain no nodes). If not empty, a binary tree has a **root node** (usually drawn at the top), and every node in the binary tree is reachable from the root node by a unique path (see Figure 7.1).

A node with neither a left child nor a right child is called a **leaf.**

An abstract data type for a binary tree should have, at a minimum, functions for creating and navigating the binary tree. For example,

- create_binary_tree(**value**, **left_child**, **right_child**)

- add_left_child(**node**, **value**)

- add_right_child(**node**, **value**)

DOI: 10.1201/9781003625506-7

- get_left_child(**node**)

- get_right_child(**node**)

- get_value(**node**)

- set_value(**node**, **value**)

- is_leaf(**node**)

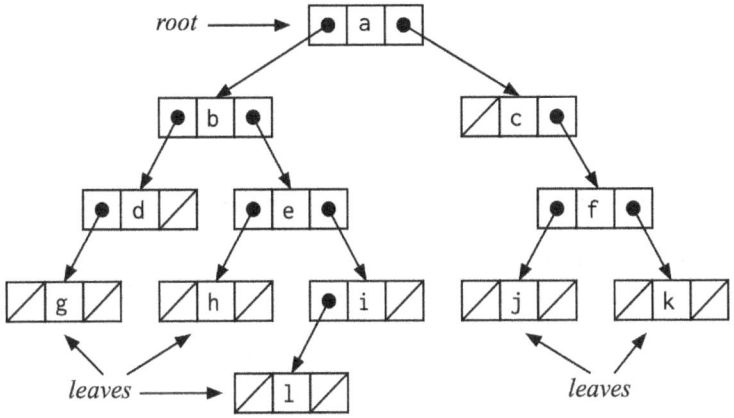

FIGURE 7.1   A binary tree.

These functions all take 0(1) time, and their names are self-explanatory. Any additional binary tree functions can be built from this set.

Here is some additional terminology:

- Node A is the *parent* of node B if node B is a child of A.

- Node A is an *ancestor* of node B if there is a path from A to B.

- Node B is a *descendant* of A if A is an ancestor of B.

- Nodes A and B are *siblings* if they have the same parent.

- The *size* of a binary tree is the number of nodes in it.

- The ***depth of a node*** is its distance from the root.

- The ***depth of a binary tree*** is the depth of its deepest node.

    Note: One thing binary trees do not usually have or need is a link from each node "upwards" to its parent. Such a link can be added if needed by the application.

Here are some important but less obvious definitions (see Figure 7.2):

- A binary tree is "full" or *complete* if there is no place to add a node without increasing the level of the tree (see Figure 7.2a).

- A binary tree of depth k is ***balanced*** if the subtree down to depth k-1 is complete (see Figures 7.2a, c, and d).

- A binary tree is ***balanced and left-justified*** if it is balanced and all the leaves at the deepest level are as far to the left as possible (see Figure 7.2d).

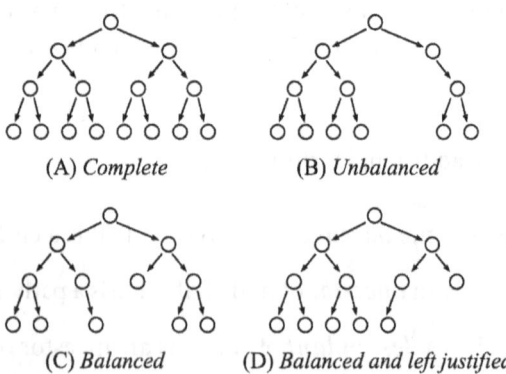

(A) *Complete*　　　　(B) *Unbalanced*

(C) *Balanced*　　(D) *Balanced and left justified*

FIGURE 7.2　Types of binary trees.

7.1 BINARY TREE TRAVERSALS

A binary tree is defined recursively: it consists of a root, a left subtree, and a right subtree. To **traverse** (or walk) the binary tree is to visit each node in the binary tree exactly once. Tree traversals are naturally recursive.

Since a binary tree has three "parts," there are three possible ways to traverse the binary tree in a forward direction. These are named according to when the root is visited.

- **Preorder**: Root, left subtree, right subtree.

- **Inorder**: Left subtree, root, right subtree.

- **Postorder**: Left subtree, right subtree, root.

One way to visualize these traversals is to attach a "flag" to each node. For preorder, the flags go on the left of each node; for inorder, on the bottom of each node; and for postorder, on the right of each node. To traverse the binary tree, simply collect the flags (see Figure 7.3).

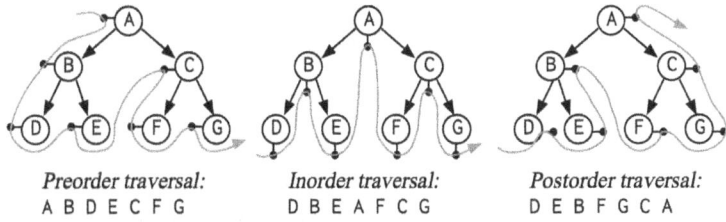

Preorder traversal:
A B D E C F G

Inorder traversal:
D B E A F C G

Postorder traversal:
D E B F G C A

FIGURE 7.3   Binary tree traversals.

There are three additional ways to traverse a binary tree; these are simply the reverses of the forward traversals.

- **Reverse preorder**: Root, right subtree, left subtree.

- **Reverse inorder**: Right subtree, root, left subtree.

- **Reverse postorder**: Right subtree, left subtree, root.

Most operations involving binary trees are best done recursively. For example, here is how to use a preorder traversal to make a copy of a binary tree.

```
function copy_tree(node):
    If node is null, return null.
    root = create_leaf(copy(node)).
    left = copy_tree(get_left_child(node)).
    right = copy_tree(get_right_child(node)).
    return new binary_tree(root, left, right)
```

7.2 BINARY SEARCH TREES

A **binary search tree** is a binary tree such that, for each node, the value in the node is greater than all the values in its left subtree and less than all the values in its right subtree. Such a binary tree is said to be **sorted** (see Figure 7.4 for two examples).

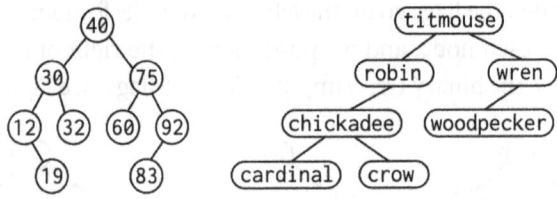

FIGURE 7.4   Binary search trees.

To insert a value into a binary search tree, compare its value to the value at the root node. If the new value is less, insert it into the left subtree; if greater, insert it into the right subtree. If the chosen subtree is absent, place the new value in that location.

Deletion of a value from a binary search tree is usually not implemented. If this operation is needed, Figure 7.7 ("Reheaping") suggests how to go about it.

As the name implies, binary search trees are used primarily for fast lookup. If the tree is balanced, lookups (and insertions) are

O(log n). Other fast operations include finding the smallest value, finding the largest value, and performing an inorder traversal to get all the values in ascending order.

If a search tree is not balanced, lookups and insertions will take more than O(log n) time. In the worst case, if the values are inserted in ascending (or descending) order, all left subtrees (or all right subtrees) will be absent. This will result in O(n) insertion and lookup times.

7.3 TREE BALANCING

For efficiency, we would like our binary trees to be balanced. Insertions can unbalance a tree; in this section, we will show the simplest (but not the most efficient) technique for rebalancing a tree.

Consider any node in the tree. If its left subtree is deeper than its right subtree, we can perform a ***right rotation*** (Figure 7.5, going from left to right). If the node's right subtree is deeper than its left subtree, we can perform a ***left rotation*** (Figure 7.5, going from right to left).

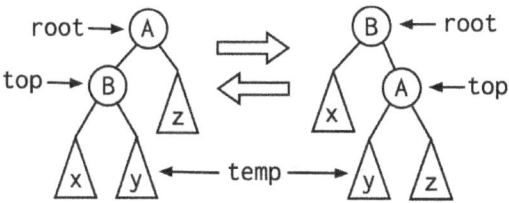

FIGURE 7.5   Binary tree rotations.

In Figure 7.5, A and B are individual nodes with specific values, while the triangles marked x, y, and z represent complete subtrees containing any number of nodes.

Consider the tree on the left, with A at the root. Since we are considering binary search trees, all the values in x are smaller than any other values in the tree, and all the values in z are larger than any other values. Of more interest, the values in y are all less than A but greater than B.

We can perform a **right rotation** as follows: B keeps its left subtree x, and A keeps its right subtree z, but A becomes the root of a right subtree of B (allowable because A > B), and y becomes a new left subtree of A (allowable because the values in y are all greater than B but less than A). The inverse operation, left rotation, also maintains the sorted order of the binary search tree.

As a check, notice that inorder traversals of the two trees in Figure 7.5 produce identical results: x-B-y-A-z.

To rotate right:

```
top = left child of root.
temp = right child of top.
right child of top = root.
left child of root = temp.
Use top as the new root.
```

To rotate left:

```
top = right child of root.
temp = left child of top.
left child of top = root.
right child of root = temp.
Use top as the new root.
```

Multiple rotations may be required to completely rebalance a binary search tree. One way to do this is to traverse the tree in postorder, performing rotations as required. The efficiency of this method depends in part on how expensive it is to determine the depth of individual nodes.

For very large binary search trees, simple rotations may be too inefficient. There are more efficient techniques, such as *red-black trees* and *AVL trees*, but these are complex and (in the opinion of this author) not worth committing to memory.

7.4 HEAPSORT

Heapsort is a well-known, traditional sorting algorithm that any student of data structures would be expected to know. It is generally slower than quicksort but has the advantage that its running time is always $O(n^2)$, so it is safer in time-critical situations. In addition, it's a really interesting algorithm.

We'll explain heapsort in three stages. First, we'll talk about building a binary tree. Second, we'll show how that binary tree can be mapped into an array. Third, we'll show how rearranging values in the binary tree is equivalent to sorting the array.

We need two definitions:

- A node in a binary tree has the *heap property* if the value in the node is *at least as large as* the values in its children. (Leaves, having no children, automatically have the heap property.)

- A binary tree is a *heap* if every node in it has the heap property.

  Note: The word "heap" is also used to denote a large area of memory from which the programmer can allocate blocks as needed and deallocate them (or allow them to be garbage collected) when no longer needed (see Chapter 9). This is a completely unrelated meaning of the word "heap."

We'll begin by building a binary tree, one node at a time.

In a binary tree, a node has links to its children, but (in most implementations) it has no link to its parent. We will just be talking about a binary tree, not implementing one, so we can ignore that limitation.

7.4.1 Phase 1: Heapifying a Binary Tree

To begin, consider a binary tree with only one node. This node has no children; therefore, it has the heap property, and the entire binary tree is a heap.

Next, consider adding a node to a binary tree (of whatever size) that is a heap. For reasons that will be apparent later, we will add the node next to the leftmost node in the bottom level or, if that level is full, as the leftmost node in a new level. The result will be a binary tree that is balanced and left-justified.

There are two cases: (1) The value in the new node may be smaller than or equal to the value in its parent. In this case, the parent node retains the heap property, and nothing more needs to be done. (2) The value in the new node may be larger than the value in its parent, in which case the parent no longer has the heap property, and we need to *sift up* (see Figure 7.6).

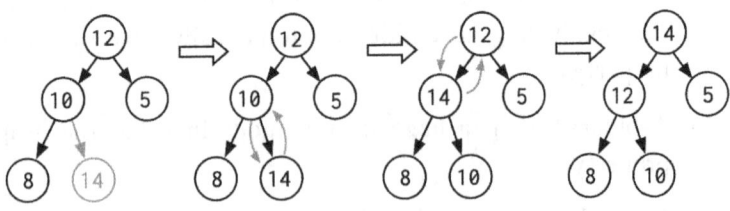

FIGURE 7.6   Sifting up.

In Figure 7.6, the binary tree is initially a heap, but then a node containing 14 is added to it. Since 14 is greater than 10, these two values must be exchanged. But then 14 is less than 12, so these two values must be exchanged. This process continues up the tree, possibly as far as the root.

After sifting up, all nodes in the binary tree again have the heap property. This is because the values in all the affected nodes (except the one in the leaf) can only increase, so the values in those nodes are still at least as large as either of their children. The only node to have its value reduced is the newly added leaf, which has the heap property because it's a leaf.

When all the values to be sorted have thus been added to the binary tree, the tree is a heap. It isn't sorted—values seem to be somewhat randomly arranged—but the largest value is at the root.

Now it gets weird.

7.4.2 Phase 2: Removing the Root and Reheaping

Once our hypothetical binary tree has been completely built, we will do something that we would never do with an actual binary tree: We *remove the root*, resulting in (in the general case) two disconnected binary trees, each of which is a heap.

To repair the damage, we will remove the rightmost node in the bottom level of the tree and use it to replace the old root node. This gives a binary tree again, but the root node may not, and probably does not, have the heap property. We need to **reheap** the binary tree (see Figure 7.7).

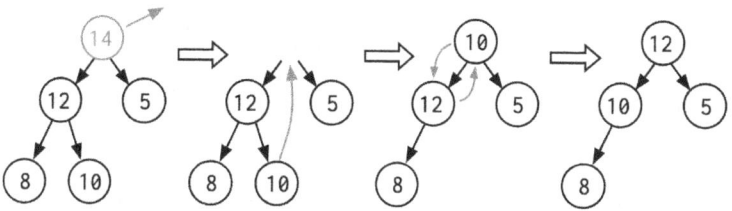

FIGURE 7.7   Reheaping.

To reheap the binary tree, exchange the value in the root node with the value in one of its two children, whichever is larger. (If they are equal, choose either.) This restores the heap property of the node at the root, but the chosen child may or may not have the heap property. If it does not, exchange its value with that in the larger child; and so on, down the binary tree, until the value that was in the root reaches a position where it again has the heap property.

By repeatedly removing the root and reheaping the binary tree, we get a series of steadily decreasing (or at least, non-increasing) values, so we have the conceptual basis of a sorting technique. To turn this into an actual sorting technique, we need to put the binary tree into an array and work with it there.

7.4.3 Phase 3: Mapping a Binary Tree into an Array

There is an obvious way to put a binary tree into an array. Put the root value into the first location, then put the values of its left and right children in the second and third locations. Next, put the values of the root's grandchildren into the array, then the great-grandchildren, and so on (see Figure 7.8).

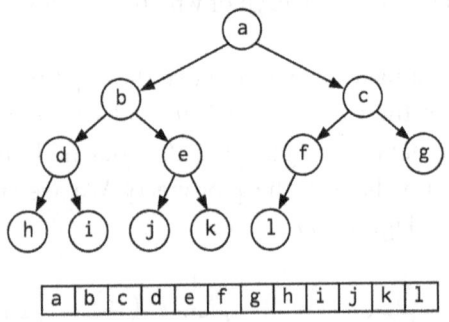

FIGURE 7.8 Array representation of a balanced, left-justified binary tree.

This mapping of binary trees to arrays works *only* when the binary tree is balanced and left-justified. If it isn't, there will be "holes" in the array that don't correspond to nodes, and these would have to be marked in some way.

There are simple formulas for finding the left child, right child, or parent of a node. They are slightly different for 0-based arrays and 1-based arrays.

If the first location in the array is at index 1:

- The left child of a node at location k is at 2*k.

- The right child of a node at location k is at 2*k+1.

- The parent of a node at location k is at k/2, using integer division.

If the first location in the array is at index 0:

- The left child of a node at location k is at 2*k+1.

- The right child of a node at location k is at 2*k+2.

- The parent of a node at location k is at (k-1)/2, using integer division.

Up to this point, we have only *imagined* performing the heap operations on a balanced, left-justified binary tree. Now that we have a way to represent such a binary tree as an array, we can *implement* those operations.

7.4.4 The Complete Heapsort Algorithm

Finally, here is the code to heapsort an array.

```
Heapify the array.
While the array isn't empty:
    Swap the first and last elements.
    Decrement the index of the "last" element by 1.
    Reheap the new root node.
```

All the values to be sorted are already present in the array, but we will pretend otherwise. As nodes are added to or removed from the binary tree, the values to the right become "invisible" to us. In other words, we will think of only the initial part of the array as representing the binary tree.

Here's the algorithm again, this time in words.

1. *Heapify* the array. Initially, the only value "visible" to us is the root, in the first location, so it is a leaf and has the heap property. As we step forward in the array, successive values become visible to us, and for each new value, we need to check whether its parent still has the heap property. If not, we *sift up*, exchanging values with the parent, and possibly its parent's parent, and so on. When all the nodes have thus become visible, the array is a heap, but it isn't yet sorted.

2. Repeatedly exchange the value in the root (first) location with the value in the last visible location. This is the array equivalent of removing the root and replacing it with the rightmost leaf in the lowest level of the tree. This puts the largest remaining value in the last visible location, which now becomes "invisible," that is, no longer part of the binary tree. The root location probably no longer has the heap property, so it has to be *reheaped* by comparing its value with those of its two children, and so on down into the binary tree. When the visible part of the array is reduced to a single node, the array has been sorted.

7.4.5 Analysis

In the first phase, we "add" n nodes to the binary tree. Each added node may have to be sifted up. Since the tree is balanced, the maximum depth is *log(n)*, so for each node added we may have to do as many as *log(n)* exchanges; therefore, the running time of this phase is O(n log n).

In the second phase, we "remove" n nodes (those currently at the root). Since these are replaced by nodes that probably do not have the heap property, they may have to be reheaped. The maximum depth of the binary tree is *log(n)*, so this phase also requires O(n log n) time.

Finally, O(n log n) plus O(n log n) is O(n log n).

7.5 HUFFMAN ENCODING

Huffman encoding is the data compression technique used for zip files, gif files, and others. It uses a binary tree to create the encoding.

The concept underlying Huffman encoding is entropy. **Entropy** is a measure of information content: the number of bits required to store data, rather than the number of bits typically used.

Entropy is sometimes called a measure of surprise. If you randomly choose a letter from a page of text, you won't be very surprised if you get a T or an E, but you would be more surprised if you get a J or a Q. Common letters such as T and E have lower entropy than J or Q, so they should be represented with fewer bits. Huffman encoding does this.

To create an encoding for text, the first step is to find the frequencies of each character. (For photographs, we might do the same for pixels.) Letter frequencies for English can be found in numerous sources and vary slightly according to the text used; in the following example, we use some of the values from https://pi.math.cornell.edu/~mec/2003-2004/cryptography/subs/frequencies.html.

Construction of the tree is quite simple. Make a list of the leaves and their associated frequencies. At each step, the two smallest values in the queue are removed, a new (non-leaf) node is created with the sum of these values, and placed back in the list. (A **priority queue**, described in Chapter 8, is ideal for this purpose.)

For a small example using only eight characters, see Figure 7.9.

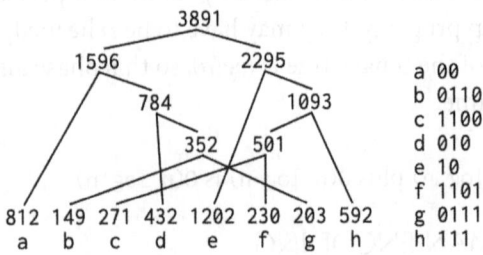

FIGURE 7.9   Huffman encoding.

The encoding for each character is determined by the path from the root to that character, using 0 for the left child and 1 for the right child. For example, d is encoded as 010, and the word decade as 0101011000001010.

Text encoded in this way can be decoded because the codes have the **unique prefix property**: None of the resultant binary codes is a prefix of any other code. This property holds because, in a binary tree, a leaf is not on a path to any other node.

Using the above encoding, the entropy of English text is about 4.7 bits/character. This can be considerably improved by using digraphs (letter pairs), trigraphs (letter triples), whole words, or even larger units. For whole words, the entropy measure drops to about 2.62 bits/character. Similar results can be expected for other languages that use an alphabet.

To decode a Huffman-encoded file, the code table must be included with the encoded data. This is a minor cost for large files, but for small files, the encoded file plus the code table may be larger than the unencoded file.

CHAPTER **8**

Priority Queues

A QUEUE IS A LAST-IN, last-out data structure. A *priority queue*, on the other hand, returns the highest priority item first; the order of insertion makes little difference. As an abstract data type, a priority queue could be defined to have the following operations:

- **Create** a new, empty priority queue.

- **Add** an item with a given priority to the priority queue.

- **Look at** the highest priority item.

- **Remove and return** the highest priority item.

- **Test** if the priority queue is empty.

This isn't the only way an ADT (abstract data type) could be defined for a priority queue. For example, the test for whether a priority queue is empty could be replaced by a function that returns the number of elements it contains. As another example, instead of the priority being inherent in the element to be added, it could be assigned when the element is added. And, of course, many additional operations could be added.

DOI: 10.1201/9781003625506-8

The point is that there is not one universally agreed-upon way to define an ADT. Rather, what is important is that the programmer defines *some* fixed set of operations for a data structure and prohibits others by hiding the implementation.

8.1 PRIORITY QUEUE IMPLEMENTATIONS

There are numerous ways a priority queue could be implemented. It could be done with

- An unsorted array. Insertion time would be $O(1)$, removal time would be $O(n)$.

- A sorted array. Insertion time would be $O(n)$, removal time would be $O(n \log n)$.

- An unbalanced (random) binary tree. Depending on implementation, insertion and deletion times would range from $O(1)$ to $O(n)$.

- A balanced binary tree. Insertion and deletion times would both be $O(\log n)$, and rebalancing the binary tree after each operation would take an additional $O(\log n)$.

The last of these is the fastest implementation; the disadvantage is that binary tree balancing algorithms are complicated. We will consider a simpler but in some ways equivalent implementation, using a **heap** (see Section 7.4).

In the heapsort algorithm, an array can be used to represent a *left-justified balanced binary tree* (defined in Chapter 7). In such an array, there are simple formulas that can be applied to the array index of a node to find the indices of that node's parent, left child, and right child. As the algorithm runs, it repeatedly generates the largest remaining value in the array.

With that reminder, here's how to implement a priority queue:

- Define an array with enough capacity to hold as many values as can occur in the priority queue at any one time. (This requires judgment or the use of an array such as Python's "list" that has flexible bounds.) Be sure to test for overflow.

- To insert a value, put it at the end of the current values in the array, and then *sift up* until that value is in its proper place.

- To get and remove a value, return the value in the first location (the "root"), replace it with the value in the last location, and *reheap*.

This works if the "highest priority" is represented by the largest number. Frequently, however, the highest priority is often represented by the *lowest* number, with priority 1. This requires a redefinition of "**heap property**."

To heapsort an array into ascending order, we defined the heap property of a node to be that the value in the node is at least as large as the values in its children. If we instead define the heap property to mean "at least as small," then the heapsort will sort an array into descending order. In a priority queue, this change will result in always returning the smallest numeric value, that is, the one with the highest priority.

CHAPTER 9

Heaps

A s shown in Section 5.1.3, all modern programming languages use a stack to keep track of local variables. Local variables and parameters are added to the stack when a function is entered and removed from the stack when the function exits. This works fine for fixed-size values such as numbers and pointers.

Larger items, such as arrays, nodes, and strings, are kept in a *heap*. As an abstract data type, the heap has only two fundamental actions: (1) *allocate* a block of storage of a given size from the heap and return a pointer to it, and (2) *deallocate* a block of storage—that is, recycle it by returning it to the heap.

Some languages make it the responsibility of the programmer to allocate and deallocate storage, while other languages allocate storage automatically as needed and use *garbage collection* (see Section 9.3) to recycle it afterward. Either way, the storage is on a heap.

DOI: 10.1201/9781003625506-9

9.1 HEAP IMPLEMENTATION

A *heap* is a single large block of storage, perhaps a few megabytes, to be parceled out and used as needed. Heaps are used by every programming language that allows new objects or arrays to be created during program execution.

A *block* is a single, contiguous area of storage within the heap. It has a *header* containing at least two items of information: a pointer to another block and the size of the block. The pointer is used to organize blocks into a singly linked list, and the size needs to be known when the block is deallocated. See Figure 9.1.

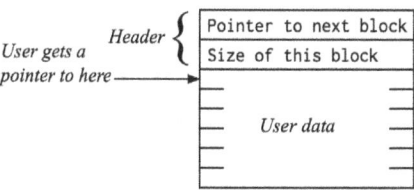

FIGURE 9.1   Single node used for a heap.

Initially, the entire heap consists of a single block, and the system has a pointer (let's call it free) to that block. We will fill up the heap from the far end (the end farthest from the header).

To allocate a block of size n:

- Find an unused block in the heap that has at least n+2 storage locations available.

- Use the n+2 locations at the end of the block we just found to create a new block, and reduce the size of the block it was taken from by n+2.

- Set the size of the new block. The pointer field is not used.

- For security reasons, zero out the user data area of the block.

- Give the user a pointer to the new block.

Figure 9.2 (1) shows the state of the heap after A has been allocated, and then B, and then C. Note that the blocks may be of different sizes. After each allocation, the size of the free block is decreased.

In Figure 9.2 (2), the block assigned to A has been deallocated. The free pointer points to this newly deallocated block, while the pointer in the block is assigned the previous value of free. This begins a linked list of deallocated blocks.

In Figure 9.2 (3), the block assigned to C has been deallocated. Pointers have been updated to maintain a list of deallocated blocks.

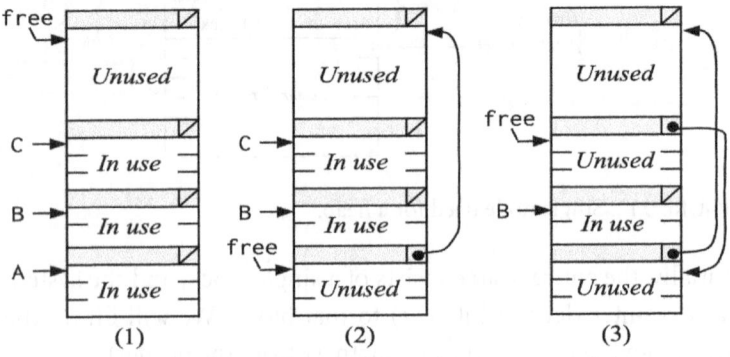

FIGURE 9.2   Heap before and after allocations and deallocations.

Under heavy use, heaps are subject to a problem called *fragmentation*. While there may be enough *total* free space to allocate a large block, that space is in fragments—consisting of small blocks scattered throughout the heap.

To deal with fragmentation, contiguous free blocks may be *coalesced*. In Figure 9.2 (3), the topmost unused area and the adjacent one pointed to by free could be combined into a single, larger block. The algorithm for doing this, which we will only hint at here, involves sorting the links to unused blocks by storage address.

A more effective approach to dealing with fragmentation is to pack all the blocks in active use into one end of the heap. This can't be done if the user has pointers to the active blocks, but it is possible if the user is only given *handles* (pointers to pointers) to the active blocks. This allows the actual block pointers to be updated as the blocks are moved. After this, all unused blocks will be contiguous and can be coalesced into one large block.

9.2 DEALLOCATION PROBLEMS

There are two potential errors when deallocating (freeing) storage.

A block may be deallocated too soon, while it is still accessible to some variable (let's call it x) in the program. Then the block may be allocated and used to hold some other, unrelated data. The variable x then becomes a *dangling reference*—it points to the wrong kind of data, and using x to modify that data could have serious consequences.

The other kind of error occurs when storage is no longer in use but isn't deallocated, causing the heap to gradually fill up with inaccessible data. This is called a *memory leak*; if the program runs long enough, it will fail with an "out of memory" error.

These errors are common in languages that leave allocation and deallocation up to the programmer; they are much rarer in languages that perform *garbage collection* (see Section 9.3).

If you have to deallocate storage yourself, a good strategy is to keep track of which function or method "owns" the storage. The function that owns the storage is responsible for deallocating it. Ownership can be transferred to another function or method; you just need a clearly defined policy for determining ownership. In practice, this is easier said than done.

9.3 GARBAGE COLLECTION

Garbage is storage that has been allocated but is no longer available to the program. It's easy to create garbage: (1) Allocate some storage and save the pointer to it in a variable. (2) Assign a different value to that variable.

A *garbage collector* automatically finds and deallocates garbage. This is far safer (and more convenient) than having the programmer do it. Dangling references cannot happen, and memory leaks, while not impossible, are much less likely.

Practically every modern language, not including C++, uses garbage collection. While it is unlikely that you will ever need to write a garbage collector, it can be helpful to understand how they work.

There are two well-known algorithms (and several less well-known ones) for performing garbage collection: *Reference counting* and *Mark and sweep*.

9.3.1 Reference Counting

When a block of storage is allocated, it includes header data that contains an integer *reference count*. The reference count keeps track of how many references (pointers) there are to that block.

When a pointer to the block is duplicated and saved in a new variable, the reference count is incremented. If a variable is changed to no longer point to the block, the reference count is decremented. If the reference count reaches zero, no remaining program variables point to it, and it can immediately be garbage collected.

Reference counting is a simple technique that is occasionally used. However, it is unreliable. If object A contains a pointer to object B, and object B contains a pointer to object A, then each is referenced, even if nothing else in the program references either one.

Circular references such as this will fool the garbage collector, which won't collect either object A or object B. The result is a memory leak.

9.3.2 Mark and Sweep

When memory runs low, languages that use **mark and sweep** temporarily pause the program and run the garbage collector.

First, the garbage collector marks every block. (Blocks must have a field in the header for this purpose.)

Second, the garbage collector performs an exhaustive search, starting from *every* reference variable in the program, and unmarks all the storage it can reach. When it finishes, every block that is still marked must not be accessible from the program; it is garbage that can be freed.

For this technique to work, it must be possible to *find* every reference variable. This can't be done by searching the raw code; instead, each time a reference variable is created, its location must be recorded, probably in a linked list. This is additional overhead.

Mark and sweep is much more reliable than reference counting, but it takes substantial time and, unlike reference counting, it must be done all at once—nothing else can be going on. The program stops responding during garbage collection. This can be a problem for many real-time applications.

CHAPTER 10

Trees

A **TREE** IS LIKE A binary tree, except that each node may have any number of children. To emphasize the distinction, a tree is sometimes called a **general tree**.

The usual way to implement a tree is with nodes containing three fields: some data value, a link to a list of children, and a link to the next sibling. See Figure 10.1.

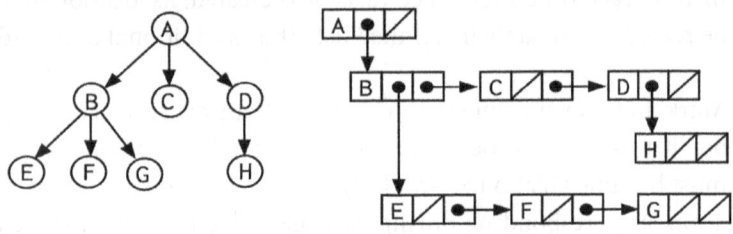

FIGURE 10.1   A general tree and its implementation.

Most of the terminology used to describe binary trees (ancestor, sibling, depth, etc.) can also be used for general trees, and there are a few additional terms:

   DOI: 10.1201/9781003625506-10

- An *ordered tree* is one in which the order of the children is important; an unordered tree is one in which the order doesn't matter, and the children of a node can be thought of as a set.

- The *branching factor of a node* is the number of children it has.

- The *branching factor of a tree* is the average branching factor of its nodes.

Branching factors can be important when determining the Big-O running times of tree algorithms.

To define a tree as an abstract data type, the following operations must be defined:

- **Construct** a new, possibly empty tree.

- **Add** a child to a node.

- **Iterate** through the children of a node, or (if ordered) **get** the ith child of a node.

- **Get** and **set** the value in a node.

If **node removal** is permitted, that usually means deleting the entire subtree whose root is that node.

General trees can be traversed in preorder: Visit the root and then traverse each child. Similarly, general trees can be traversed in postorder: Traverse all the subtrees, and then visit the root. Inorder traversals are not well defined.

10.1 APPLICATIONS OF TREES

In this section, we discuss some of the most common applications of trees.

10.1.1 File Systems

File systems are almost always implemented as a tree structure. The nodes in the tree are of (at least) two types: **folders** (also called **directories**) and plain files. Folders are nodes that may themselves have children, while plain files do not.

A folder also contains a link to its parent, usually indicated by two dots (..). In UNIX, the root of the tree is denoted by a forward slash (/); in Windows, the root is probably denoted by C:.

10.1.2 Family Trees

Family trees are a challenge to represent accurately. If we ignore such factors as adoption, there are two basic problems. First, each person represented has two parents. Second, people often have children with more than one partner.

One approach to overcoming these problems is to have, in addition to nodes representing individuals, nodes representing marriages (or affairs). It gets complicated.

A better way to represent biological relationships is with an "upside down" binary tree so that the root is a single individual. Since it is a biological fact (so far) that every child has exactly two biological parents, we can use left child = mother and right child = father. The terminology gets a bit confusing, since "parent" and "child" have opposite meanings in a binary tree than in a family.

This approach can easily be extended to multiple individuals. Suppose you have an extensive family tree with some individual at the root. A related individual could then have a "mother link" (left child) to a node in that binary tree, a "father link" (right child) to a node in that tree, or both, or neither. In this way, subtrees could be **shared** between individuals. To complete the data structure, you could add a list of "root" individuals, forming a "forest" of binary trees.

However, such "biological family trees" are probably only useful for medical/genetic purposes. To properly represent the wide variations in "societal family trees" (with adoptions, remarriages, same-sex marriages, etc.), some other data structure must be used, and it won't be as simple as a tree.

10.1.3 Game Trees

Trees are used heavily in implementing games, particularly board games.

A node represents the state of the game at one point in time. For example, if the game is chess, the state would include the positions of all the pieces, whose turn it is, and whether check has been called.

Each possible move represents a single step from the current node. The branches from a node represent the possible moves; the children represent the new positions. Planning ahead (in a game) means choosing a path through the tree.

A complication arises if it is possible to return to an earlier state of the game, allowing players to repeat the same sequence of moves over and over, resulting in a game that never terminates.

One way to handle a repeated state is to ignore the fact that it has occurred previously and treat it as a new node in the usual fashion. In theory, this would result in an infinitely deep tree and could lead to an infinite loop when choosing a path through the tree. This might or might not be a problem—if a tree is being built, it is built as needed, so an infinitely large tree would not be built. Similarly, deciding on a move (i.e., determining which child node to go to next) almost always involves a *limited* search, since finding a path all the way through to the end of the game is infeasible for any game much larger than tic-tac-toe.

Another way to handle a repeated state is to give a node a link back up in the tree to one of its ancestors. While this isn't exactly illegal, it violates the definition of a "tree," and the result is more properly called a **graph** (see Chapter 11) and should be treated as such.

10.1.4 Expressions

When a program is compiled, the first step is almost always **parsing** the program. Parsing creates a tree structure that is equivalent in meaning to the text of the program.

In the resultant **parse tree**, a node that is a leaf could hold either a value or the name of a variable whose value could be looked up (e.g., in a hash table). A node that is not a leaf could hold the name or symbol for an operation to be applied to the values of its children.

Control statements (while, if, etc.) are considered to be just another kind of operator. For example, the statements "First assign 1 to m; then while m is less than 1000, multiply m by 2" can be represented as shown in Figure 10.2; the sequencing operation is represented by a semicolon so that A;B means "first do A, then do B."

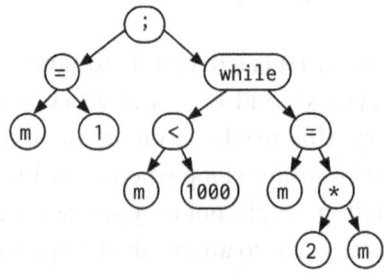

FIGURE 10.2 Tree representation of code.

While you may never be called upon to write a compiler, anything that has syntax—dates, addresses, phone numbers—can be parsed into its components. If you can't parse text inputs, you are limited to reading simple things like numbers and strings. But if you *can* parse text input, you can make sense of:

- `tell Mary "Meet me at noon"`
- `fire phasers at 3, 7`
- `jane.doe@google.com`
- `28°12"48'`
- `3:30pm-5pm`

One simple approach, which we won't go into any detail here, involves two phases. In the first phase, the code breaks the input into a list of tokens, for example, `["3", ":", "30", "pm", "-", "5", "pm"]`. In the second phase, the next operator is found, suitable operands are looked for in the list of tokens, and those are assembled into a tree structure.

10.2 TREE SEARCHING

A *tree search* starts at the root and explores nodes from there, looking for a *goal node* (a node that satisfies certain conditions, depending on the problem). Figure 10.3 shows a small tree with two goal nodes, K and O, as indicated by double circles.

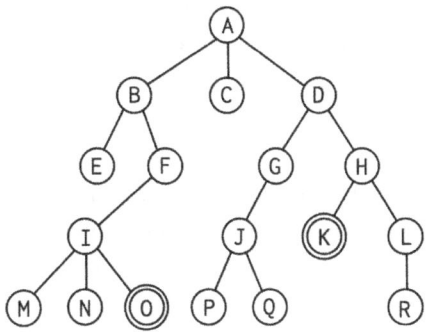

FIGURE 10.3   A tree with goal nodes marked.

For some problems, any goal node is acceptable (K or O); for other problems, you want a minimum-depth goal node, that is, a goal node nearest the root (only K).

A *depth-first search* (*DFS*) explores a path all the way to a leaf before *backtracking* (going back to a previous node and exploring from another child of that node).

In the example tree, after visiting A (the root), the search proceeds to B, and then to E. The search then backtracks to B and searches from F, which leads to I, then M, and then successive backtracking to I leads to N and finally to O. Since O is a goal node, the search is complete.

A *breadth-first search* (*BFS*) explores nodes nearest the root before exploring nodes further away. In the example tree, a BFS would first visit A (the root), then B, C, and D, then E, F, G, and H, and finally I, J, and the goal node K.

10.2.1 Depth-First Searching

To perform a depth-first search (DFS) of a tree:

```
Put the root node on a stack.
While the stack is not empty:
    Remove a node from the stack.
    If the node is a goal node, report success.
    Put the children of the node onto the stack.
Report failure.
```

At each step, the stack contains some nodes from several levels. The size of the stack required depends on the branching factor b. While searching level n, the stack contains approximately b × n nodes.

When this method succeeds, it returns some goal node but doesn't report the path taken to it.

To perform a *recursive* depth-first search,

```
function search(node):
    If node is a goal, return success.
    For each child c of node:
        If search(c) is successful,
            save the node, and
            report success.
    Return failure.
```

The stack only needs to be large enough to hold the deepest search path.

When the function succeeds, the (implicit) stack contains only the nodes on a path from the root to a goal. As the recursion "unwinds" through multiple levels, those nodes can be saved in some external data structure, such as a stack.

If a goal node nearest the root is required, depth-first searching is inappropriate. It may find an arbitrarily deep goal node rather than a nearby one. It can also fail if there are extremely deep paths not containing a goal node.

10.2.2 Breadth-First Searching
To perform a breadth-first search (BFS) of a tree:

```
Put the root node on a queue.
While the queue is not empty:
    Remove a node from the queue.
    If the node is a goal node, report success.
    Put all children of the node onto the queue.
Report failure.
```

The advantage of a breadth-first search is that when it succeeds, it finds a minimum-depth (nearest the root) goal node.

Breadth-first searching has some serious disadvantages.

- In a typical tree, the number of nodes at each level increases exponentially with the depth. During the search, the queue will hold, at various times, *all* the nodes at a given level. Hence, memory requirements may be infeasible.

- A successful breadth-first search doesn't provide the path to the goal node, and there is no recursive equivalent that will give the path.

- For a large tree, a breadth-first search may take an excessively long time to find even a very nearby goal node.

10.2.3 Depth-First Iterative Deepening

Depth-first searches have reasonable memory requirements but may overlook nearby goal nodes. Breadth-first searches find nearby goal nodes but may require excessive memory. A *depth-first iterative deepening search* has both advantages: it will find nearby goal nodes while using a reasonable amount of memory.

We first consider **depth-limited searching**. This is just a recursive depth-first search with a counter to limit how deep the search goes.

```
function limitedDFS(node, limit, depth):
    If depth > limit, return failure.
    If node is a goal node, return success.
    For each child of node:
        If (limitedDFS(child, limit, depth + 1))
            Save node on an external stack.
            return success.
    Return failure.
```

Since this method is basically DFS, when it succeeds, the path to a goal node can be recovered by pushing the current node onto a stack just before the return success statement.

We can now use this function to perform a ***depth-first iterative deepening search.***

```
limit = 0.
found = false.
While not found:
    found = limitedDFS(root, limit, 0).
    limit = limit + 1.
```

This code searches to depth 0 (root only), then if that fails, it searches to depth 1 (root and its children), then if that fails, it searches to depth 2 (root and its children and grandchildren), and so on.

Like BFS, if a goal node is found, it is a nearest node, and the path to it is on the stack.

Like DFS, the required stack size is only the search depth (plus 1).

One apparent disadvantage is that when doing a limited DFS to depth n, all the previous work (to depth n-1, n-2, etc.) is simply discarded. While true, this is less of a waste than it may appear. When searching a binary tree to depth 7, a single DFS requires searching 255 nodes, while iterative deepening requires searching 502 nodes. In general, iterative deepening takes about twice as long. With a tree that has a branching factor of 4, DFS to depth 7 requires searching 21845 nodes, while iterative deepening searches 29124 nodes—about 4/3 = 1.33 times as long.

The higher the branching factor, the lower the relative cost of iterative deepening DFS. In general, if the branching factor is b, the difference is about b/(b-1).

10.2.4 State-Space Searches

Some problems are best represented as a search in a state space. A *state space* consists of a (possibly infinite) set of *states* and a set of *operators*.

The *start state* represents the initial problem. Applying an operator to a state in the state space transforms it to another state in the state space. Some states may be *goal states*; these represent solutions to the problem.

Not all operators are applicable to all states.

Example 1: Maze

A maze can be represented as a state space. Each state represents "where you are" in the maze. The start state represents your starting position, and the goal state represents the exit from the maze.

Operators (for a rectangular maze) are: move north, move south, move east, and move west. Each operator takes you to a new state, which is simply your location in the maze. Operators may not always apply because you are not allowed to walk through walls.

See Section 11.8 for an example of a rectangular maze.

Example 2: Sliding Blocks

One of the best-known sliding block puzzles is the *fifteen puzzle*. It contains 15 tiles, numbered 1 through 15, in a 4x4 grid. The start state is some apparently random configuration of the tiles, while the goal state is one where the numbered tiles are in order; see Figure 10.4.

Note: In the fifteen puzzle, only half the possible configurations are reachable from (or to) the goal state. If the state space is thought of as an undirected graph, it has two distinct connected components. Hence, the start state cannot be completely random.

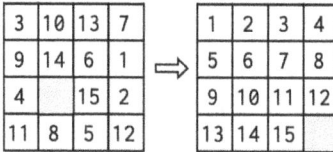

FIGURE 10.4   The fifteen puzzle, unsolved and solved.

In this problem as in many others, the choice of operators is critically important. This choice affects both execution time and the difficulty of writing the code.

The obvious set of operators is to move an individual block either left, right, up, or down. As there are 15 blocks, this results in a total of 60 operators, at most four of which will be applicable from any given state. This isn't ideal.

A much better set of operators is to move the *space* either left, right, up, or down. Of these four operators, at least two will be applicable from any given state.

We will return to this puzzle in Section 11.9.1.

Example 3: Angels and Demons

"Missionaries and cannibals" is a classic puzzle, but to avoid giving offense to any cannibals among my readers, I have recast it as "angels and demons." (Besides, this simplifies finding appropriate images.)

Here's the problem. Three angels and three demons want to cross a river. They have a canoe that will hold only one or two at a time (see Figure 10.5). Unfortunately, if at any time the demons outnumber the angels, they will destroy the angels. How do you get everyone safely across the river?

We will explore the state space of this problem in somewhat more detail.

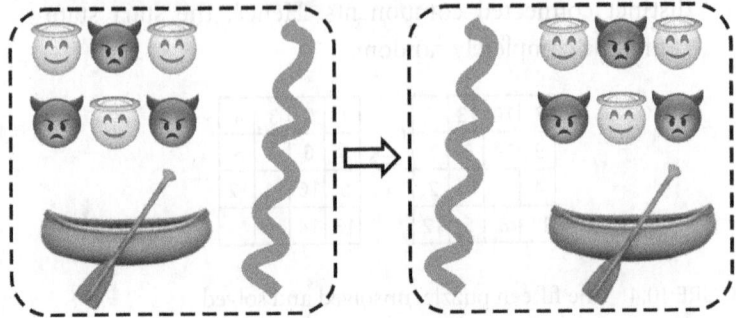

FIGURE 10.5 Angels and demons—start state and goal state.

We need to represent the possible states, preferably in as simple a manner as possible. A triple of numbers is enough: The number of angels on the left bank, the number of demons on the left bank, and the number of canoes (zero or one) on the left bank.

We will define five possible operations, named a, d, aa, dd, and ad:

- a: Use the canoe to take 1 angel across the river.
- d: Use the canoe to take 1 demon across the river.
- aa: Use the canoe to take 2 angels across the river.
- dd: Use the canoe to take 2 demons across the river.
- ad: Use the canoe to take 1 angel and 1 demon across the river.

We don't have to specify "west to east" or "east to west" because only one of these will be possible at any given time.

Figure 10.6 shows the initial portion of a state-space search for this problem. The search space continues after the vertex in the bottom right.

In Figure 10.6, each node shows in the top line what is on the left bank and (redundantly) in the bottom line what is on the right bank. This redundancy does not need to be reflected in the code; it's in the figure to make it easier to see

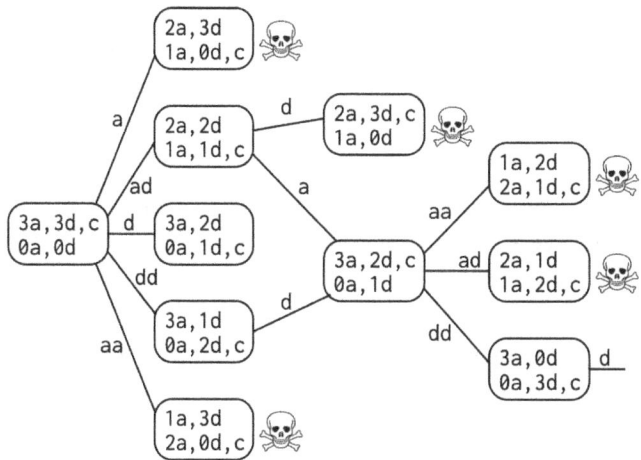

FIGURE 10.6   Initial part of the search space for angels and demons.

when demons outnumber angels. A *failure node* (marked with a skull and crossbones) occurs when demons outnumber angels on either bank.

The search space is shown as an undirected graph. Most edges may be traversed in either direction; the exception is that there is no exit from a failure node. Because there are cycles in the graph, graph searching techniques (see Section 11.4) are appropriate.

10.2.5 Pruning

In any kind of search, *pruning*—deleting (or just ignoring) subtrees that cannot contain a goal node—can save considerable effort. For very large search trees, it may also be advisable to prune subtrees that seem unlikely to contain a goal node so that more promising subtrees may be searched to a greater depth.

Pruning is important because the savings in time can be exponential. Consider a binary search tree: If one of the two children of the root can be pruned, search time is cut in half. Each of the four grandchildren that can be pruned will save one-quarter of the time. And so on. The higher in a tree that pruning occurs, the greater the savings.

10.2.6 Alpha–Beta Searching

In many tabletop games, such as chess, checkers, and backgammon, two players take turns choosing moves. This complicates the search for a winning move.

Because such games result in very large search trees, it is generally not possible to search deep enough to find a winning node, so heuristics are used to evaluate the "goodness" of nodes. The idea of an **alpha–beta search** is to prune branches that are unlikely to be taken, thus allowing deeper searches on more promising branches.

An **alpha cutoff** occurs when it is your move, and you decide not to explore certain subtrees because you have already found a more promising subtree of that node. A **beta cutoff** occurs when it is your opponent's move, and you believe that your opponent will not move into that subtree because it is more desirable to you.

Figure 10.7 shows the result of an alpha–beta search on a tree that is just barely big enough to show some examples. Your moves are

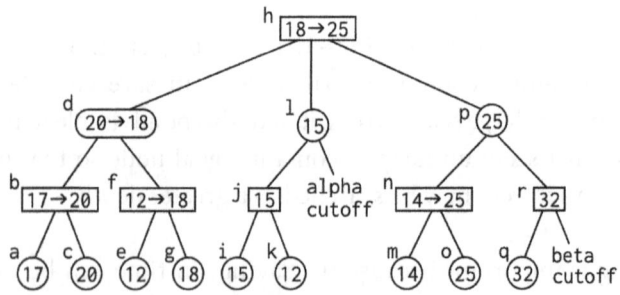

FIGURE 10.7   Alpha–beta cutoffs.

shown as rectangular nodes; your opponent's moves are shown as round or rounded nodes.

a. The search extends down to node a, which has a heuristic value of 17.

b. The value 17 is brought up to node b. This is known as a *preliminary backed-up value* (*PBV*); it can change.

c. The next child of node b, node c, is evaluated. It has a heuristic value of 20.

b. Since 20 is better than 17, the PBV at b is replaced by 20.

d. A PBV of 20 is brought up to node d.

e. From node d, we explore down to node e, which has a heuristic value of 12.

f. Node f is assigned a PBV of 12.

g. Node g is visited, and it has a heuristic value of 18.

f. The PBV of 12 at node f is replaced by the better value of 18.

d. Node d is the opponent's move, so they will replace the PBV of 20 with the (better for them, worse for you) value of 18.

h. The PBV of 18 is brought up to node h.

i, j, k, l. Node l is explored, and gets a PBV of 15. But 15 is worse than the parent node's PBV of 18, and your opponent will never bring up a larger value; therefore, there is no point in exploring any further subtrees of l. This is an alpha cutoff, and the value of 15 is *not* brought up to node h.

m, n, o, p. The leftmost child of p is explored, and p gets a PBV of 25.

q, r. Nodes q and r are explored, and a PBV of 32 is brought up to node r. But 32 is worse for your opponent than the PBV of 25 at p, so the value of 32 is not brought up, and a beta cutoff occurs.

h. The PBV of 25 at node p is better than the PBV of 18 at node h, so it replaces the value in node h.

According to what has been determined so far, you should move from h to p, your opponent will likely move from p to n, and you should move from n to o. However, after your opponent's move, you will probably have an opportunity to do another, deeper search and very likely get some different values.

More explicitly, an alpha cutoff occurs when:

- It is your *opponent's* turn to move, and
- You have computed a PBV for this node's parent, and
- The node's parent has a *higher* PBV than this node, and
- This node has other children you no longer need to consider.

A beta cutoff occurs when:

- It is *your* turn to move, and
- You have computed a PBV for this node's parent, and
- The node's parent has a *lower* PBV than this node, and
- This node has other children you no longer need to consider.

Alpha–beta searching assumes that your opponent has the same heuristic function as you (i.e., they assign the same heuristic values to nodes). This is probably an incorrect assumption, but better heuristics and deeper searches tend to win out over weaker heuristics and shallower searches.

10.3 TRIES

A *trie* is a data structure used for storing and re*trie*ving a very large collection of strings—say, a complete lexicon or a large number of DNA nucleotide sequences.

The trie in Figure 10.8 represents 15 words: a, an, and, any, than, that, the, there, these, those, what, when, where, who, and why. Black nodes indicate that a complete word has been formed at that point. To locate a given word, start at the root and follow the link labeled with the first letter; then follow the link labeled with the second letter; and so on.

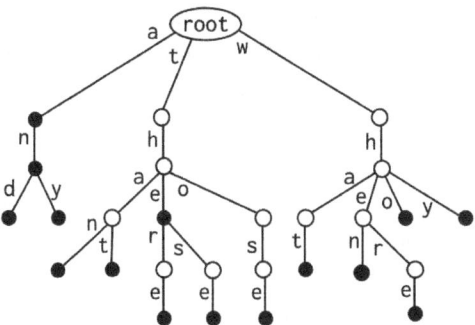

FIGURE 10.8   A trie.

Conceptually a trie is a kind of tree, but the implementation is completely different. Instead of linked lists, tries use arrays. In our example, we will discuss a trie containing all and only English words that can be formed using the 26 lowercase letters. Figure 10.9 shows a part of the implementation of the trie in Figure 10.8; ellipses indicate parts that have been omitted from the figure.

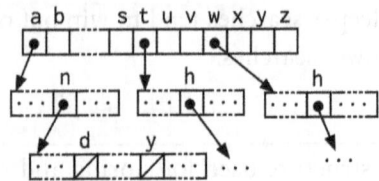

FIGURE 10.9   Part of the trie implementation.

At the root of our example trie is an array of 26 locations, corresponding to the 26 lowercase letters. Each array contains two things: a link to a sub-trie and a Boolean (not shown in Figure 10.9) indicating whether a complete word has been formed.

Letters are not explicit in the trie; they are implied by locations in the array. The first location of the root array contains a link to a sub-trie for all words beginning with 'a,' the second contains a link to a sub-trie for words beginning with 'b,' and so on. Each sub-trie has the same form, with links to its own sub-tries.

To look up the word 'any,' start in the root array and follow the link in the first location (a); from the array that link points to, follow the link in the fourteenth location (n); from that array, follow the link in the twenty-fifth location (y). This is a leaf, so a-n-y is a word. (So are 'a' and 'a-n,' but as they are not leaves, those array locations must contain a Boolean to indicate they are also complete words.)

> **Note:** To convert letters to numeric indices, subtract the numeric value of 'a' from the numeric value of the letter; add 1 if your arrays are 1-based.

Tries have a large number of advantages.

- Tries are extremely efficient in terms of execution time.
  - The time required to build a trie is O(nk), where n is the number of strings and k is the average length of a string.

- Insertion, deletion, and lookup each require only O(k) time.

- Words can be looked up in O(L) time, where L is the length of the word; non-words may require even less time.

- The complete word list can be generated in alphabetical order using a preorder traversal.

- Tries can be used to find words with a given prefix, which can be useful for auto-completion, for example.

It may seem that the space complexity required for a trie could be exponential. In theory, a trie using 26 letters might require 26 raised to the power of the maximum word length. However, in practice, the space required is limited to a constant times the actual number of strings. While this may represent a substantial amount of storage, it isn't exponential.

A trie can also be represented using hash maps instead of arrays. This approach has the advantage of supporting a flexible set of characters (e.g., Unicode) rather than a fixed-size set, but it loses the ease of generating all words (or other types of strings) in alphabetical order.

CHAPTER 11

Graphs

A **GRAPH** IS A DATA structure that consists of a collection of *vertices* connected by **edges**. There are two kinds of graphs: **directed graphs** (sometimes called **digraphs**) and **undirected graphs** (see Figure 11.1). Edges in a digraph can be followed only in one direction, while edges in an undirected graph may be followed in either direction.

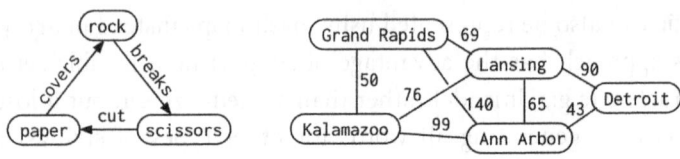

FIGURE 11.1   Directed (left) and undirected (right) graphs.

Since edges in a graph are often represented by pointers or references that can only be followed in one direction, edges in an undirected graph are often implemented by a *pair* of pointers, one in each direction.

In a graph, data is usually (but not necessarily) stored in the vertices. As shown in the graphs in Figure 11.1, data may also be stored in the edges.

DOI: 10.1201/9781003625506-11

There are many ways to implement graphs. But first, some terminology.

- The *size* of a graph is the number of vertices it contains. The *empty* graph has no vertices, so its size is zero.

- If two vertices are connected by an edge, they are *neighbors*, and the vertices are *adjacent* to each other.

- The *degree* of a vertex is the number of edges it has.

- For directed graphs,

  - If a directed edge goes from vertex S to vertex D, we call S the *source* and D the *destination* of the edge.

  - An edge from S to D is an *out-edge* of S and an *in-edge* of D. S is a *predecessor* of D, and D is a *successor* of S.

  - The *in-degree* of a vertex is the number of in-edges it has, while the *out-degree* of a vertex is the number of out-edges it has.

- A *path* is a list of edges such that every vertex but the last is the predecessor of the next vertex in the list.

- A *cycle* is a path whose first and last vertices are the same (e.g., [rock, scissors, paper, rock]).

- A *cyclic graph* contains at least one cycle, while an *acyclic graph* does not contain any cycles.

- An undirected graph is *connected* if there is a path from every vertex to every other vertex.

- A directed graph is *strongly connected* if there is a path from every vertex to every other vertex, and *weakly connected* if the underlying undirected graph (ignoring edge direction) is connected.

- Vertex X is **reachable** from vertex Y if there is a path from Y to X.

- A subset of the vertices of a graph is a **connected component** (or just a **component**) if there is a path from every vertex in the subset to every other vertex in the subset.

The best way to implement a graph depends on how the graph is to be used; here are some questions to consider:

- How large is the graph?

- Is data associated with the vertices? With the edges?

- Should vertices be ordered? How about the out-edges of a vertex?

- Which graph operations need to be efficient?

11.1 GRAPH APPLICATIONS

Graphs can be used for

- Finding a route to drive from one city to another

- Finding connecting flights from one city to another

- Determining least-cost highway connections

- Designing optimal connections on a computer chip

- Implementing automata

- Implementing compilers

- Doing garbage collection

- Representing family histories

- Doing similarity testing (e.g., for a dating service)

- Pert charts

- Playing games

- Finding a minimum-length path.

11.2 ADJACENCY MATRIX REPRESENTATIONS

An adjacency matrix is a particularly simple way to represent a graph because it uses a matrix, or two-dimensional array. Figure 11.2 shows an example of a directed graph and its representation as a matrix.

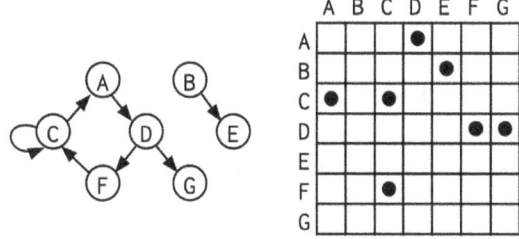

FIGURE 11.2   Matrix representation of a directed graph.

If there is an edge from vertex i to vertex j, then there is a value in row i and column j of the array. In a Boolean array, an edge can be represented by True and the absence of an edge by False. If the array is numeric, array entries can be used to represent values on the edges (miles from city A to city D, for example).

This representation shows connections between vertices but does not support storing data in those vertices. If that is needed, it must be done elsewhere.

An undirected graph can be represented in the same manner. If there is an edge between vertex i and vertex j, then there is a value in row i and column j of the array, but *also* in row j and column i (see Figure 11.3).

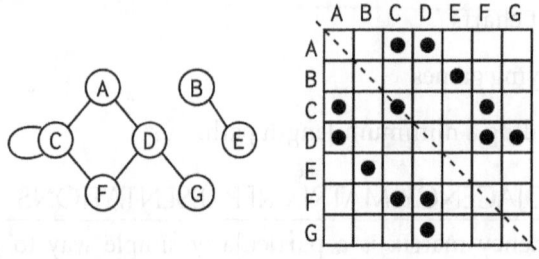

FIGURE 11.3 Matrix representation of an undirected graph.

The adjacency matrix for an undirected graph is symmetric about the main diagonal, as shown in Figure 11.3. Each edge is represented by two marks, except in the special case where an edge goes from a vertex back to the same vertex.

For very dense graphs—ones in which there are edges between almost every pair of vertices—matrix representations may be appropriate. However, adjacency matrices require $O(n^2)$ space to represent n vertices, regardless of the number of edges. For less dense graphs, this disadvantage can be overcome by the use of a **sparse array** (see Section 11.5).

11.3 REPRESENTATION BY SETS

In this section, we will explore graph implementations using sets of vertices and sets of edges.

> **Reminder:** A **set** is an unordered collection of values in which each value occurs either exactly once or not at all. By convention, set values are shown enclosed in curly braces, {}.

Many languages provide sets as a built-in data type. If not, they can be implemented, perhaps as a hash table. Our focus in this section will be on using sets, although if an ordering is desired, lists can be used instead.

An *edge set* implementation of a directed graph is just a set of edges, where each edge is a pair of values (link to source vertex and link to destination vertex) and possibly a value for the edge itself. If desired, the vertices themselves can be in a second set.

To represent an undirected graph, the two vertices of an edge can be treated as the two ends of the edge, rather than source and destination.

The main advantage of an edge set representation is that it is easy to implement. It also makes it easy to find vertices from an edge, but finding the edges from a vertex requires searching the set of edges. This makes finding a path from one vertex to another very inefficient.

An *adjacency set* implementation makes a graph much more navigable by including redundant information: An edge "knows about" its source and destination, while a vertex "knows about" its out-edges (and possibly its in-edges) (see Figure 11.4).

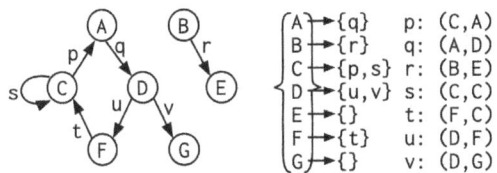

FIGURE 11.4   Adjacency set representation of a graph.

If the edges p through v have no associated values, they can be elided. Each vertex, instead of pointing to a set of edges, can point to the set of vertices reachable by following those edges.

11.4 SEARCHING A GRAPH

With certain modifications, any tree search technique can be applied to a graph. This includes depth-first, breadth-first, depth-first iterative deepening, and almost any other type of search. The difference is that a graph may have cycles, and any search technique must avoid getting caught in endless repetitions around a cycle.

To avoid getting trapped in a cycle, keep track of which vertices you have already searched, so you don't repeat those searches. There are two ways to do this: (1) keep a list of vertices you have already visited, or (2) put a mark on the vertices you have visited. The latter approach is more intrusive—it might interfere with later searches—and in a team setting, you may not have the option to change how vertices are implemented.

We will compare the code for performing a depth-first search (DFS) on a tree with doing the same kind of search on a graph. Other types of searches require similar changes.

Here is how to do DFS on a tree:

```
Put the root node on a stack.
While the stack is not empty:
    Remove a node from the stack.
    If the node is a goal node,
        return success,
    else
        put all children of the node onto the stack.
If you get to here, return failure.
```

Here is how to do DFS on a graph:

```
Put the starting vertex on a stack;
While the stack is not empty:
    Remove a vertex from the stack.
    If the vertex has already been visited,
        continue with the next loop iteration.
    If the vertex is a goal node,
```

```
        return success,
    else,
            put all the successors of the vertex
                onto the stack.
If you get to here, return failure.
```

You can use DFS to find the connected components of an undirected graph. For each vertex in the graph, if it isn't already in some component, create a new component for it, then perform a DFS, and add every reachable vertex to the same component. The result will be a set of components, that is, a set of sets of vertices.

The same approach does not work for finding connected components of a directed graph. To do that efficiently requires an algorithm (Union-Find) not covered in this book.

11.5 SPARSE ARRAYS

A university or college might have thousands of students and thousands of courses. During their college career, a typical student will take perhaps a few dozen courses, get a grade in each of these, and will *not* take thousands of other courses. Suppose we represent this as an array with one row for each student and one column for each course; the student's grades would be the values in the array. If an ordinary array is used, the waste of storage space would be phenomenal. Processing times would also be negatively affected.

For this and similar situations, a *sparse array* is appropriate. As an abstract data type, a sparse array can be used just like an ordinary array, but the implementation only allocates space for non-null (or non-zero) elements.

Consider the ADT (Abstract Data Type) for an ordinary two-dimensional array. There are really only two necessary operations: (1) given the row and column indices of an array location, **store** some value in that location, and (2) given the row and column indices, **fetch** the value from that location.

To implement these two operations for a sparse array, you could use a **hash map** (see Section 3.4), using some combination of the indices to compute a hash code. That works, but it turns out to make access to rows and columns very difficult.

Returning to the college example, you might ask: What courses has this student taken? or, Which students have taken this course? With a hash map representation, these would be very difficult questions to answer. In terms of an array, these questions are equivalent to finding all the non-null values in a row and finding all the non-null values in a column.

For each row, you can use a linked list. Each node in the linked list will contain the column number (which would be hard to find otherwise) and the value (grade) in that location of the array. You could then create a linked list of these "row lists." Similarly, you can create a linked list of all the values in a column (along with their row numbers) and make a linked list of these.

Figure 11.5 shows a sparse array with both a list of "row lists" and a list of "column lists." Since a node can be approached from either direction (row or column), it should contain both the row number and the column number, along with whatever other value it may hold.

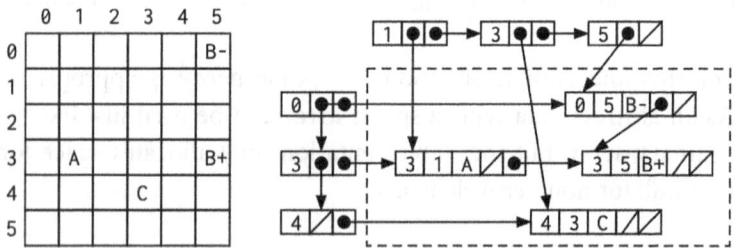

FIGURE 11.5   A sparse array and its representation.

If, as in the college example, you can expect almost every row and every column to contain some meaningful values, you can use an array instead of a list to hold links to the "row lists," and another array of links for the "column lists."

Sparse arrays are also useful in linear algebra, where you may have large matrices with almost all zero entries.

11.6 DIJKSTRA'S ALGORITHM

Dijkstra's algorithm finds the least-cost path in a graph from a given vertex to all reachable vertices. It is a complex algorithm, but is included in this book because many problems require finding a least-cost path.

Dijkstra's Algorithm builds a kind of "inverse tree," where all paths lead to the root rather than from the root. To find the best path from vertex X to some vertex Y in this tree, we start at Y and follow the only available path back to X.

Each edge in the graph has a cost (or distance) measure on it. For the algorithm to work, no edges can have a negative cost.

For each vertex V, we need to keep track of three pieces of information:

- The cost of the best path to V that has been found so far.

- Whether the cost of the best path to V is final or is still only tentative. Initially, all costs are infinite (or some suitably large number) and tentative.

- A link (directed edge) from that vertex. Initially, all links are null.

We also need to keep a priority queue of vertices adjacent to the vertices that have been visited so far.

For the graph in Figure 11.6, begin by putting vertex X into the priority queue. The cost to get to X from itself is zero, that cost is final, and the directed edge is null. Then, at each step:

1. Pull from the priority queue the vertex N with the smallest tentative cost and mark that cost as final. (Any other path to N must cost more because it must go through a vertex with a higher tentative cost.)

2. Add to the priority queue any vertices adjacent to N that are not already in the priority queue and whose cost is still tentative. Add links from each of those vertices back to N.

3. For each vertex V adjacent to N that does not already have a final cost, compute the cost of getting to V by way of N (the cost of N plus the cost of the edge from N to V). If this cost is less than the tentative cost of V, update V's tentative cost, and make it link back to N.

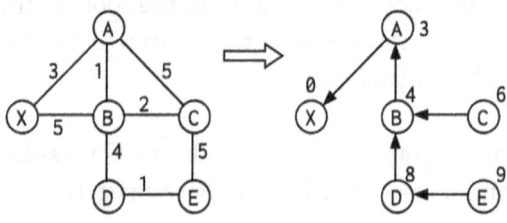

FIGURE 11.6   Dijkstra's algorithm.

When the priority queue becomes empty, all vertices reachable from X have been processed and the "inverse tree" is complete.

11.7 SPANNING TREES

A *spanning tree* of a connected, undirected graph is a connected subgraph that includes all the vertices, but only enough of the edges to maintain connectivity. It will have one fewer edge than vertices and no cycles.

To find a spanning tree of a graph,

- Pick an initial vertex and call it part of the spanning tree.

- Do a search from the initial vertex.

- Each time you find a vertex that is not in the spanning tree, add both the new vertex and the edge you followed to get to it to the spanning tree.

A graph typically has many possible spanning trees; the ones you find depend on the type of search you do. Figure 11.7 shows (a) an initial graph, (b) one possible spanning tree after a breadth-first search, and (c) one possible spanning tree after a DFS.

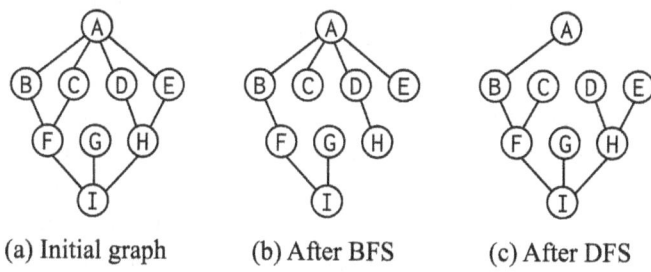

| (a) Initial graph | (b) After BFS | (c) After DFS |

FIGURE 11.7   Initial graph and two spanning trees.

Suppose you want to supply a set of houses (say, in a new subdivision) with electric power, water, sewage lines, telephone lines, and internet. To keep costs down, you might want to connect some of these (such as water and sewage) with a spanning tree.

However, the houses are not all equal distances apart, and longer pipes cost more, so you might want to use a ***minimum-cost spanning tree***. The cost of a spanning tree is the sum of the costs of its edges.

There are two basic algorithms for finding minimum-cost spanning trees, and both are greedy algorithms (see Section 13.4).

Kruskal's algorithm ignores the vertices. It starts with no edges in the spanning tree and repeatedly adds the cheapest edge that does not create a cycle. As the algorithm progresses, multiple disconnected edges join up. When the correct number of edges have been added, the result is a minimum-cost spanning tree.

Kruskal's algorithm sounds simple. However, efficient testing for the existence of a cycle requires a complex algorithm (Union-Find) which is beyond the scope of this book.

Prim's algorithm starts with putting any one vertex into the spanning tree and creating a set of edges adjacent to that vertex. The main loop then consists of taking the cheapest edge from that set and testing whether the vertex to which it leads is already in the spanning tree. If so, the edge is discarded; otherwise, it and the new vertex are added to the spanning tree, and the edges from that vertex are added to the set of edges. The algorithm ends when the correct number of edges (or vertices) are in the spanning tree.

An edge of the lowest cost can be found with a priority queue, and testing for a cycle is automatic. This makes Prim's algorithm far simpler to implement than Kruskal's algorithm.

If some redundancy is desired in a network, so that the graph remains connected when a single edge is removed, a spanning tree is not the best solution. Instead, a single cycle connecting all the vertices might be a better choice. The problem of finding such a cycle with the least cost is called the ***traveling salesman problem*** and is exponentially difficult.

11.8 MAZES

Typically, every location in a maze is reachable from the starting location, and there is only one path from start to finish. If the locations are "vertices" and the open doors between cells are "edges," this describes a spanning tree (see Figure 11.8a).

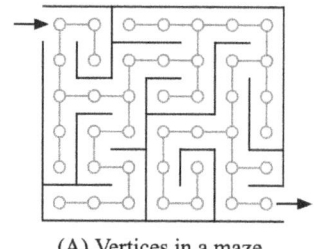

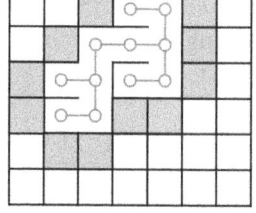

(A) Vertices in a maze   (B) Building the maze

FIGURE 11.8   Building a maze.

Since there is exactly one path between any pair of cells, any cells can be used as the "entrance" and "exit." Often, both entrance and exit are to the outside of the maze, but it is also common for one or the other to be near the center of the maze.

There is an easy way to turn a rectangular array into a maze. It requires keeping track of two sets: The set of locations already in the spanning tree (call it TREE) and the set of locations not yet in the spanning tree but adjacent to some location in the spanning tree (call it ADJ).

```
Start with all walls present.
Define two sets, ADJ and TREE, initially empty.
Set X to any array location and add it to TREE.
While there are still locations not in TREE:
    Add to ADJ all the cells adjacent to X that
        aren't in either ADJ or TREE.
    Set Y to any cell from ADJ and put it in TREE.
    Erase the wall between Y and any adjacent
        location X that is in ADJ.
```

It usually works well, when selecting the next cell from ADJ, to choose one randomly.

Figure 11.8b shows a partially completed maze. The locations containing an open circle are in TREE, and the shaded locations are in ADJ.

11.9 HEURISTIC SEARCHING

Search spaces can be very large, or even infinite. It is important to make searching as efficient as possible.

All the previous searches have been *blind searches*: They make no use of any knowledge of the problem. If we know something about the problem, we can usually do much better by using heuristics.

A *heuristic* is a "rule of thumb" for deciding which choice might be best. There is no general theory for finding heuristics because every problem is different. The choice of heuristics depends on knowledge of the problem.

This is the basic search algorithm:

```
Put the start node into OPEN.
    While OPEN is not empty:
        Take a node N from OPEN.
        If N is a goal node, report success.
        Put the children of N onto OPEN.
    Report failure.
```

If OPEN is a stack, this is a depth-first search; if OPEN is a queue, this is a breadth-first search; and if OPEN is a priority queue sorted according to most promising first, we have a *best-first search*.

If the search space is a graph that contains cycles, provision must be made to avoid searching from any given vertex more than once.

11.9.1 Solving the Fifteen Puzzle

In this section, we develop a heuristic for solving the fifteen puzzle that was described earlier in Section 10.2.4 (see Figure 11.9). Our states are the possible arrangements of tiles, and our operations are moving the blank (by sliding an adjacent tile into it) in one of four directions.

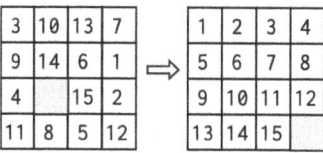

FIGURE 11.9 Fifteen puzzle (repeated image).

For any given state, we can compute an estimate of the number of moves required to reach the goal state. This will be our *heuristic measure*—the smaller the measure, the more desirable the state. The goal state itself will have a heuristic measure of zero (no moves required).

To compute the heuristic measure: For each piece, count how many moves it would take to move the piece into its proper position if no other pieces were in the way. Do this for every piece and add up the counts. The result is a (very) optimistic measure of how many moves it will take to solve the puzzle.

> **Note:** The distance covered to get from one point to another when only horizontal and vertical moves are allowed, is called the *Manhattan distance*.

In Figure 11.9, the 3 is two moves from its proper location; the 10 is two moves away; the 13 is five moves away; and so on.

With this heuristic, we can perform a best-first search.

- Create a priority queue to hold the states of the puzzle along with their heuristic measures.

- Initialize the priority queue with the start state and its heuristic measure.

- As long as the priority queue isn't empty,

  - Take the state with the best heuristic measure from the priority queue and call it the current state.

  - Find the adjacent states by making all possible moves from the current state. For each adjacent state that has not been visited previously, compute its heuristic measure and add it to the priority queue.

The search space is a graph, so it is important to avoid getting caught in a cycle.

The number of possible arrangements of the tiles is 16!, but only half of these are reachable from the goal node, so there are 16!/2 = 10,461,394,944,000 states in the search space. Even our simple heuristic measure leads to a very quick solution.

11.9.2 The A* Algorithm

The simple form of a ***best-first search*** keeps a set of nodes to explore and uses a heuristic function (applied to each of those nodes) to decide which node to explore next.

The ***A**** (or ***A-star***) algorithm is a best-first search with the additional feature that the distance already traversed (from the root to each node) is added to the heuristic function.

Let $g(N)$ be the distance from the start state to node N. Let $h(N)$ be a heuristic estimate of the distance from node N to a goal node. Then, $f(N) = g(N) + h(N)$ is the (partially known and partially estimated) distance from the start node to a goal node (see Figure 11.10).

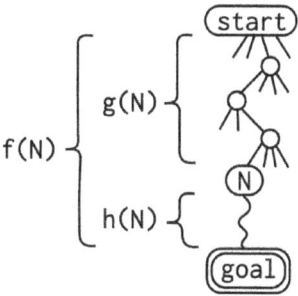

FIGURE 11.10   A* algorithm: f(N)=g(N)+h(N).

Memory requirements of A* depend on the quality of the heuristic function.

- If h(N) is a constant (it supplies no useful information), then A* is identical to a breadth-first search, and requires memory exponential in the branching factor.

- If h(N) is a perfect estimator, memory requirements will be minimal because A* will go straight to a goal with no searching required.

The quality of the solution also depends on h(N). It can be proved that if h(N) is *optimistic* (never overestimates the distance to a goal), then A* will find an optimal solution, that is, one that has the shortest path to a goal.

In the previous section, our heuristic for the fifteen puzzle was (very) optimistic; therefore, an A* search will find a solution with the fewest possible moves.

11.9.3 IDA*

In the worst case (that is, with a poor heuristic), A* is equivalent to a breadth-first search and will require exponential storage. Iterative deepening, which was described in Section 10.2.3, can be applied to the A* algorithm.

Iterative deepening uses depth-limited searching, where the search only proceeds to a fixed depth; at each iteration, the depth limit is increased. *Iterative-deepening A* (IDA*)* is just like iterative deepening, but instead of using g(N) (the actual depth so far) to limit searching, it uses f(N) (the estimated total depth).

IDA* gives the same results as A*; however, because IDA* is essentially a DFS, storage requirements are linear in the length of the path, instead of exponential in the branching factor.

The best searches combine a basic blind search technique with heuristic knowledge about the problem space, and A* and its variations, especially IDA*, are the best heuristic search techniques known.

CHAPTER 12

Hypergraphs

T HERE IS NO GENERALLY accepted definition of a hypergraph. Perhaps the best that can be said is: A *hypergraph* is a collection of zero or more graphs, generalized in some way. In this section, we will discuss some extreme generalizations, followed by an implementation.

Consider the following sentence: "John thinks Martha is a Martian." Figure 12.1 shows a hypergraph that captures this but remains neutral on the question of whether Martha is really from Mars.

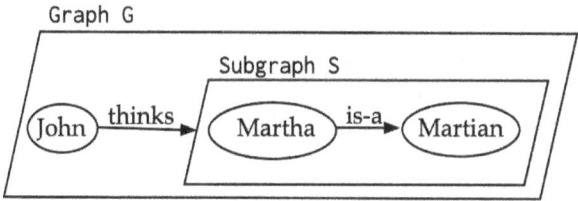

FIGURE 12.1   "John thinks Martha is a Martian."

The elements of a graph are vertices and edges, while the elements of a hypergraph are vertices, edges, *and graphs*.

DOI: 10.1201/9781003625506-12

Now consider how a hypergraph like this might be generalized by using *sets* instead of single values.

- Other people might also think Martha is a Martian, so the "thinks" edge could have a *set* of sources, rather than just one.

- This probably isn't the only thing John thinks, so "thinks" could have a *set* of targets (destinations).

- Vertices (and graphs, and even edges) might belong to a set of graphs.

Other generalizations are possible. In Figure 12.1, a graph rather than a vertex is the *target* of an edge, so it seems reasonable to allow a graph to also be a *source* of an edge. Probably less useful, but still conceivable, the source or target of an edge might be another edge.

Finally, there is no reason to restrict the sources and targets of an edge to all be in the same graph.

12.1 PLEXES

We can represent arbitrarily complex hypergraphs by means of a simple data structure called a ***plex***. A plex consists of some user data (e.g., "John") and four sets of plexes.

A plex is multipurpose: It can represent a graph, a vertex, or an edge. The four plex sets that it contains are

- **containers**: The plexes that "contain" this plex. For example, a graph may be a container for vertices and edges.

- **contents**: The plexes "contained in" this plex. For example, a graph may have vertices and edges as its contents.

- **origins**: The plexes "from which" this plex comes. For example, the origin (source) of an edge may be a vertex.

- **targets**: The plexes "to which" this plex goes. For example, an edge may have a vertex as its target.

There are two simple validity rules:

- If plex X is a container of plex Y, then plex Y is a content of plex X, and vice versa.

- If plex X is an origin of plex Y, then plex Y is a target of plex X, and vice versa.

Plexes allow almost anything. For example, a plex that represents an edge may have multiple sources and multiple targets. A plex that represents a vertex may belong to multiple graphs, and it may have multiple graphs within it. And so on.

The hypergraph in the previous section, "John thinks Martha is a Martian," could be represented by the seven plexes in Table 12.1. In this table, we can see, for example, that the edge "is-a" has its origin at "Martha"; therefore, "Martha" has a target of "is-a."

TABLE 12.1   "John thinks Martha is a Martian"

Plex	Containers	Contents	Origins	Targets
Graph G		John, thinks, Subgraph S		
John	Graph G			thinks
thinks	Graph G		John	Subgraph S
Subgraph S	Graph G	Martha, is-a, martian	thinks	
Martha	Subgraph S			is-a
is-a	Subgraph S		Martha	martian
Martian	Subgraph S		is-a	

The terminology can be confusing. In general, it is easy to see that an edge that goes from A to B has A as its origin and B as its termination. The consequence of the validity rules is that the out-edges of a vertex are its targets, and the in-edges are its origins.

A plex can represent a vertex, an edge, or a graph, and there is nothing inherent in the plex structure to indicate which is intended. Of course, such a field could be added.

Plex structures are extremely flexible; probably *too* flexible. They provide an example of what *can* be done with data structures, but perhaps not what *should* be done. If hypergraphs are ever actually needed for a project (which is unlikely), plexes stand ready to serve.

CHAPTER 13

Algorithm Types

ALGORITHMS THAT USE A similar problem-solving approach can be grouped together. By classifying algorithms into types, we can highlight the various ways in which a problem can be attacked.

In this section, we will consider several different types of algorithms, many of which have been seen in the earlier parts of this book.

13.1 SIMPLE RECURSIVE ALGORITHMS

A "simple" recursive algorithm is one that (1) solves the base cases directly, (2) recurs with a simpler subproblem, and (3) may do some extra work to convert the solution to the simpler subproblem into a solution to the given problem.

The factorial function and many operations on linked-lists (see Chapter 6) are examples that make simple use of recursion.

13.2 BACKTRACKING ALGORITHMS

Suppose you need to decide among various *choices,* where (1) you don't have enough information to know what to choose, (2) each decision leads to a new set of choices, and (3) some sequence of

DOI: 10.1201/9781003625506-13

choices (possibly more than one) may be a solution to your problem. **Backtracking** is a depth-first recursive search for a solution. That is, at each stage it makes a choice, and later may return to the same point and try a different choice.

Depth-first searching of a tree has been described in Section 10.2.1, and the modifications for searching a graph are described in Section 11.4.

Example 1: Solving a Maze

Given a maze, the task is to find a path from start to finish. At each intersection, you have to decide between three or fewer choices: You can go straight, you can go left, or you can go right. You don't have enough information to choose correctly, and each choice leads to another set of choices (another intersection). One or more sequences of choices will, if the maze is solvable, lead to a solution.

Example 2: Four-Coloring a Map

The **four-color theorem** states that only four colors are required to color any map so that any countries that share a border are different colors.

To color a map, try to choose a color for the n-th country (initially the first country) that isn't used by any adjacent country. If you can, and if this is the last country, report success; otherwise recursively color the next country. If you can't choose a color, report failure.

At each step, you don't have enough information to choose the correct color; each choice leads to another set of choices (or failure); and one or more sequences of choices will lead to a solution (if the map representation is correct).

Example 3: Peg Jumping Puzzle

In a peg jumping puzzle, all holes but one are filled with pegs. The only allowable moves are to jump one peg over another peg, and remove the jumped-over peg. The goal is to remove all pegs but one.

As in the other examples, you have to choose a move on the basis of incomplete information, each move leads to other possible moves, and (given a well-designed puzzle) some sequence of moves will lead to a solution.

13.2.1 Virtual Trees

There is a type of data structure called a tree. We are not using it here, but if we diagram the sequence of choices we make, the diagram looks like a tree (see Figure 13.1).

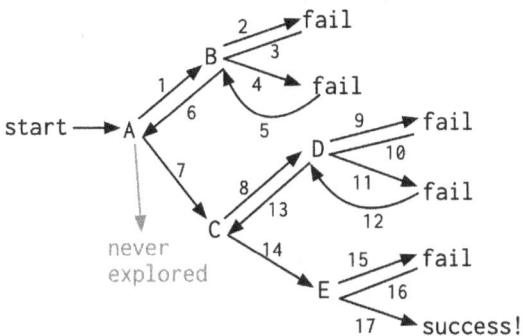

FIGURE 13.1   A virtual tree.

We search this virtual tree for a **goal node**—one that represents a solution to the problem we are trying to solve. If we reach a non-goal node from which we have no legal moves (a **failure node**), we backtrack to the most recent node that has remaining choices.

Here is a partial trace:

- Start at node A. There are three choices; follow edge 1 to B.

- From B, there are two choices. Follow edge 2 to a dead end (a failure node).

- Backtrack to node B (edge 3).

- From B, take the remaining edge, edge 4, to another failure node.

- Backtrack to B (edge 5).

- There are no more choices from B, so backtrack (edge 6) to A.

After several more moves, we follow edge 17 to a goal node, and quit with success. Had it failed, there was another choice from A, but we never needed to explore it.

13.3 DIVIDE AND CONQUER ALGORITHMS

A *divide and conquer algorithm* is one that divides a problem into two or more smaller subproblems of the same type, solves these subproblems recursively, and combines the solutions into a solution to the original problem.

Quicksort and mergesort are common examples of divide and conquer algorithms.

In quicksort, the array is partitioned into two parts and each part is sorted independently. No additional work is required to combine the two sorted parts.

In mergesort, the array is cut in half, and each half is sorted independently. Then the two halves are merged.

Binary search is sometimes called a divide and conquer algorithm. Traditionally, however, an algorithm is only called "divide and conquer" if it contains at least two recursive calls. Under this definition, binary search does not qualify.

13.4 GREEDY ALGORITHMS

A *greedy algorithm* is one in which a locally optimal choice is made at each step. The result might or might not be an optimal solution to the entire problem.

US coins come in denominations of 1, 5, 10, 25, and 50 cents. To find the minimum number of US coins to make any amount, the greedy method always works. At each step, just choose the largest coin that does not overshoot the desired amount.

For example, to make 42¢, choose the 25¢ coin, leaving 17¢. Then choose the 10¢ coin, leaving 7¢. Then choose the 5¢ coin, leaving 2¢. Then choose the 1¢ coin, leaving 1¢. Finally, choose the 1¢ coin, for a total of five coins.

The greedy method would not work if we did not have 5¢ coins. To make 42¢, the method would result in nine coins, but it could be done with six. It also would not work if, instead of removing 5¢ coins, we also had 17¢ coins.

This greedy algorithm is O(log n). It can be guaranteed to find an optimal result for some problems, but not for others.

To find the minimum number of coins for any given coin set, we need a dynamic programming algorithm.

13.5 DYNAMIC PROGRAMMING ALGORITHMS

A *dynamic programming algorithm* remembers past results and uses them to find new results.

In order to solve a problem of size k, a dynamic programming algorithm will first solve the smallest problem of that type, then the next smallest, and so on up to k. For each value of k, the solution found is saved and used at a later step.

A good first example is the **_Fibonacci series_**, introduced in Section 4.3.

```
function fibonacci(n):
    If n < 3, return 1
    else return fibonacci(n - 1) + fibonacci(n - 2).
```

This is an exponential algorithm. It makes two recursive calls at each level of the recursion, so the total number of calls keeps doubling. A dynamic programming version of this algorithm requires only linear time.

```
function fibonacci(n):
    Create an array to hold n integers.
    Set the first two array values to 1.
    For each remaining array location,
        set the array value to the sum of the
            two previous values.
    Return the value in the last array location.
```

As required by the dynamic programming approach, values of fibonacci(n) are first computed for the smallest values of n, and later values in the fibonacci series are computed from earlier values.

The reader may notice that an array isn't necessary for this problem; it can be done with only a few variables, but the resultant code is harder to understand.

As a more interesting example, we will return to the coin counting problem.

As noted earlier, the greedy algorithm finds an optimal solution for making change with American coins (1, 5, 10, 25, and 50 cents). It does not work well for every possible set of coins. For example, if the coins are 1, 3, 7, 10, and 25 cents, the greedy algorithm for 15 cents would result in one 10¢ coin, one 3¢ coin, and two 1¢ coins, for a total of four coins; a better solution is two 7¢ coins and one 1¢ coin, for a total of three coins.

We will consider two algorithms for solving the coin problem. The first is basically a divide and conquer algorithm, with terrible (exponential) running time.

```
To make K cents:
    If there is a K-cent coin,
        return 1 as the coin count for K
    Otherwise, for each value i < K,
        Solve for i cents.
        Solve for K-1 cents.
        If the sum is fewer coins for K,
            Save these two solutions.
    Return the combination of these
        two solutions.
```

Again taking the example of making 15¢ from 1, 3, 7, 10, and 25 cent coins, this would compute the best solutions for 1 and 14 cents, then for 2 and 13 cents, and so on, for all combinations that add up to 15.

If the best solution for 15¢ turns out to be 7 cents (one 7¢ coin) plus 8 cents (one 7¢ coin and one 1¢ coin), then the algorithm would combine these to get two 7¢ coins and one 1¢ coin.

This algorithm works. For 20¢, you may have to wait a bit for the answer; for 50¢, it's unfeasible.

The second solution uses dynamic programming, and it's lightning fast. The trick is to solve for one cent, then two cents, then three cents, all the way up to the desired amount. As the solution is found for each value, it is stored and never computed again.

Exactly as in the dynamic programming version, for 15 cents we compute the best solutions for 1 and 14 cents, then for 2 and 13 cents, and so on, for all combinations that add up to 15. Then, we combine the two solutions. The difference is that instead of recursively computing the solution pairs each time, we simply look them up.

```
For M from 1 to K:
    If there is an M-cent coin,
        that one coin is the minimum;
        save 1 as the coin count for M.
    Otherwise,
        Store a very large coin count for M.
        For each value i < M,
            Look up the coin counts for i cents
              and for M-i cents.
            If the sum is better than the
              saved coin count for M,
                save this as the coin count for M.
    Return the coin count for K.
```

The running time for this algorithm is O(KN), where K is the desired amount and N is the number of different kinds of coins.

Dynamic programming is generally used for optimization problems, where there are multiple solutions and the goal is to find the "best" one.

In order to use dynamic programming to solve a problem, the problem must satisfy the *principle of optimality*: the optimal solution is a combination of the optimal solutions for subproblems. Or, looking at this in reverse, if a problem has an optimal solution, it contains optimal solutions to its subproblems.

In the coin example, if the optimal way to make change for K involves making change for A and for B, where K = A + B, then that is the optimal way to make change for A and the optimal way to make change for B.

13.6 BRUTE FORCE ALGORITHMS

A *brute force algorithm* is one that tries all possibilities until a solution is found.

Whether a brute force algorithm is adequate for a given task depends on the problem size and the algorithmic complexity. Discovering a randomly generated password has exponential complexity. The traveling salesman problem (see Section 2.18) is a typical example of a problem for which the best-known solution requires exponential time.

Sum of subsets is another such problem. Suppose you are given a list or set of n positive numbers, such as [22, 26, 31, 39, 43, 56], and are asked to find a subset of the numbers that total to a certain amount, say 100. Each number either is or is not in the solution, so there are 2^n possible subsets to try—or, in this tiny example, $2^6 = 64$ subsets. Clearly, this is an exponential problem.

The binary nature of this problem (a number is either in the subset or it isn't) makes it convenient to use binary numbers in the solution. Generate the 64 6-bit binary numbers 000000 up to 111111. Multiply each number in the list by the corresponding bit value; for example, if the binary number is 110001, compute:

22*1 + 26*1 + 31*0 + 39*0 + 43*0 + 56*1 = 104

As is often the case, pruning (see Section 10.2.5) can help considerably. For example, if the count has reached 000111, the total is 138, and all remaining numbers of the form xxx111 can be ignored. Other stratagems can be employed to further reduce the number of subsets examined, but in the end, this problem remains stubbornly exponential in difficulty.

13.7 RANDOMIZED ALGORITHMS

A *randomized algorithm* uses a random number at least once during the computation to make a decision.

Technically, Quicksort could be considered a randomized algorithm if random numbers are used to choose pivot, but this is a minor use and hardly counts.

More often, randomized algorithms are used for problems in which choices must be made and there is no good way to make them. In these problems, multiple attempts are made to solve the problem, making random choices, and either a solution is found, or the program keeps track of the "best so far" solution.

Here's a real-life example from my teaching experience. I had my students doing *pair programming*—two people working together on the same assignment. For the first assignment, pairs were chosen randomly. (Assume, for simplicity, that I had an even number of students.)

For each subsequent assignment, I again wanted to assign students to pairs randomly, with the additional constraint that every student got a different partner each time. I could think of no better algorithm than choosing pairs randomly, one pair at a time, and starting over if the constraints were violated. The program was slow, sometimes taking a couple of minutes, but it got me through the semester.

Afterword

If you have finished this little volume, you have a good understanding of how data structures are constructed from three simple elements—arrays, nodes, and pointers. You have been introduced to all the most common data structures, and you can recognize the importance of Big-O running times and how to estimate them.

Few programming languages provide data structures beyond stacks, hash maps, and doubly (but not singly) linked lists. If your language has the data structure you need, use it; it is probably well debugged and efficiently implemented. You might find implementations on the Web that you can adapt and debug. Beyond that, you should now be able to create data structures as you need them—possibly ternary trees, a heap for fixed size nodes, or a priority queue for partially ordered items.

A thoughtful and informed choice of data structures will greatly improve your code, but no amount of attention to code can compensate for a poor choice of data structures. Start with the data structures you need, and the rest will follow.

Index

Note: **Bold** page numbers indicate where the term is defined.